Sweet Evenlode

Sweet Evenlode

Godfrey Hodgson

The Wychwood Press

Frontispiece: Rupert's Beach

First published in 2008 by The Wychwood Press
an imprint of Jon Carpenter Publishing
Alder House, Market Street, Charlbury, Oxfordshire OX7 3PH

Text © Godfrey Hodgson
Design: Sarah Tyzack
Photographs © Sarah Tyzack, Jon Carpenter;
on pages 25 and 26 © Richard Broughton;
on page vi © Godfrey Hodgson

ISBN 978 1 902279 31 2

Printed in England by The Cromwell Press, Trowbridge

≈ A PERSONAL PREFACE ≈

M Y SON Pierre, who lives in France and divides his
life between a farm in the fragrant limestone plateau
above the Gorges du Tarn in the Lozère and the sunbaked
hills of Provence, accuses me, more in bemusement than anything else, of having fallen in love with West Oxfordshire. I
admit the charge. As I will explain, we have lived in or close
to the Evenlode valley since we first rented what was at first
a weekend cottage and became for a time a 'principal residence' in Chastleton in 1975. After we moved to Chilson, my
daughters, Jessica and Laura, spent happy hours playing
along and in the river between Pudlicote and Ascott mill. For
them the whole valley, a good two miles square, was one out-
doors playground, and I believe that both of them have carried good memories of it with them to busy lives, one as a
journalist, one as a lawyer, in the City of London. We do not
now seriously contemplate, indeed we could hardly imagine,
living anywhere else.

For even longer, I have earned at least part of my living by
writing books about American politics and history. This very
different book came about in unusual circumstances. About a
year ago I emerged from four months in hospital. At first I
could hardly remember how to use a computer keyboard. In
those first uncertain weeks at home, hobbling around, first on
a walking frame, then on crutches, then with a walking stick

and at last, tentatively, on my own two hind legs, my friend and neighbour Jon Carpenter suggested, or perhaps it was I who first suggested to him, that I might try to write, and he would publish, this book.

I am more grateful to him than I can say for helping me, in a literary sense, from frame to the stick. It is intended as a votive offering to a landscape I love, and as an introduction that may give newcomers to this blessed place some sense of why we love it. It has been a pleasure to write, and I hope it will be read with some pleasure too.

The author, not drowning but waving, near Pudlicote bridge.

❦ ONE ❧

Sweet Evenlode run swiftly till I end my song!

TWENTY years ago the writer Claudio Magris, born in Trieste and so bilingual in Italian and German, not to mention capable of reading and conversing in Slovenian, Serbo-Croat and Hungarian, wrote a book of magisterial erudition called simply *Danube.* On the seventeen-hundred mile course of that mighty river, from the baroque fountain in the prince Fuerstenberg's garden in Donaueschingen that is supposed to mark its source, past Vienna and Budapest, under the battered fortress of Belgrade and through the rapids of the Iron Gates, to its misty mouth on the Black Sea, he threaded the whole bloody history of Middle Europe. He brought to life the literature of half a dozen languages, and also found space for learned disquisitions on the fish, the hydrology and the economics of Europe's longest river.

The Evenlode is hardly worthy to be compared with the mighty Danube, which runs through nine countries and whose tributaries are said to bring water from seven others[1] — its name in a dozen languages means simply 'the river'. To set out to chart its course and evoke its associations in comparison with such a noble model must be an essay in the mock-heroic mode. Still, like the Danube, the Evenlode has position and length; it has its own hydrological pattern, its fisheries, its literary associations, and no mean history.

1

The Danube rises in the Black Forest. (There is a healthy argument about where exactly its source is to be found. *Hier entspringt die Donau*, 'Here is the source of the Danube', says a plaque next to the baroque bowl in the prince's garden at Fürstenberg, but the villagers of Furchtwang, 48 kilometres upstream, claim that it rises there. One proud Furchtwanger poured a bottle of his village's water into the prince's fountain to prove his point. Others say it is born of the confluence of the Breg and the Brisach; while others again, in a satisfactorily *Mitteleuropa* way, assert that the Danube runs into one of its own tributaries.) Beyond question it waters the peach orchards of the Wachau, crosses the *puztas* plains of Hungary, and breaches the wall of the Carpathians.

There is no dispute over the origin of our river; it is not important enough for that. It comes together unnoticed, and wanders gently from nowhere to nowhere, through fields of yellow rapeseed and pastures green, past villages of stone-tiled cottages and church towers in Early English and Perpendicular, creating deep satisfaction to those of us who love it.

It once bisected and now bypasses the ancient royal forest of Wychwood. Between drifts of ragwort and meadowsweet, which in West Oxfordshire we more prosaically call 'keck', it provides swimming holes for a dozen villages and once drove a dozen mills. It flows from the Cotswolds to the outskirts of Oxford. It was not even the Evenlode, but the Thames, or Themmes, as he spelled it, into which it flows, that inspired Edmund Spenser to ask it to run softly.

The Evenlode is only 68 kilometres or 42 and a bit miles long, and less than that if you measure only as the crow flies, straightening all its willow-shaded meanders. (The Danube, second longest river in Europe after the Volga, is 1770 miles long.) Even at its widest the Evenlode is no more than ten metres across, and in its upper reaches you can step over it. It has no great cities on or near its banks, no Vienna or Budapest. The only substantial small town anywhere near it is Charlbury, with 3,000 people, which sits up on a low bluff a quarter of a mile away. Unlike the Danube, though, it is an ideal companion, not for furious waltzing, but for contemplative walking. We should begin, of course, with the upper reaches.

≋ TWO ≋

I T SO happens that the Evenlode has been a pleasing thread running through my own life. More than half a lifetime ago, quite by accident, my wife Hilary and I bought a cottage in Chastleton, a stone's throw from the glorious Jacobean façade of Chastleton House.[2] It was only a mile or so along a secluded lane from the upper reaches of the Evenlode. From our cottage there, we could pass the football commentator Jimmy Hill's house at Harcomb and follow a grass lane to the point where it turned away towards Moreton, then cross a couple of fields to the village of Evenlode.

Eight years later, we moved to Chilson, and from the study on the top floor of our tall stone house, Pennyfields, I could count the swans nesting on the Evenlode as it flowed under Pudlicote Bridge. After that, for a few years we moved into Oxford, and would sometimes walk along the towpath of the

Isis, as the Thames is called there, past the place where the expiring Evenlode pours its waters into the bigger river.

Finally, when I retired from my job in Oxford, we moved to the village of Finstock. There was nothing accidental about the choice. I got an ordnance map and plonked my finger down on the middle valley of the Evenlode and announced that that was where I wanted to be.

It was in Finstock that we found an undistinguished but roomy house, then only nine years old. The English of my generation do not like new houses. The meanest eighteenth-century labourer's cottage, so long as it has stone walls and if possible a thatched roof, fetches £100,000 more than a comfortable house with headroom, double-glazing and efficient central heating. Our house was unmistakably modern, and therefore unfashionable, but by way of compensation it has the space we need for children and now for grandchildren and for books, and an acre of garden running uphill where the builder, my neighbour, had failed to get planning permission to build more houses. And it had a secret attraction. Sure enough, half a mile down the leafy tunnel of Dark Lane, which starts opposite the Plough Inn, in the part of the village officially designated as The Bottom, there is the swirling water of our old friend the Evenlode again. It is guarded in summer by deep banks of nettles and rosebay willow herb, and crossed by a little bridge to take us under the brick arch of a railway viaduct to Fawler on the far bank.

≈ THREE ≈

THE EVENLODE rises, not on the highest ridge of the Cotswolds, but on the southern slope of that wave of the hills that is crowned by Stow church and runs from there to Bourton-on-the Hill above Moreton. The Cotswolds are a series of ridges. They rise from the Thames valley to the escarpment of the much more sharply defined Severn valley, a thousand feet above sea level, which runs from Cleeve Cloud Hill above Cheltenham past Birdlip and the Golden Valley to the neighbourhood of Bristol. This stretch of hill country, shaped like a cockleshell, is scored by a series of pretty little rivers converging on the Thames, among them Churn, Coln, Windrush, Evenlode, Glyme and Cherwell.

The streams that come together to form our river rise in Gloucestershire near Moreton-in-Marsh and for a while it is the boundary between Gloucestershire and Oxfordshire. The higher western edge of the Evenlode's catchment area has relatively heavy rainfall, over 800 mm or 32 inches a year, while the middle Thames Valley, where it ends, has no more than 650 mm or some 26 inches a year. In its upper reaches and in its faster flowing tributaries the channel is narrow. In the higher reaches, where the surrounding land is largely clay, the run-off is quick and the river is 'flashy', prone to flash floods: sometimes the river runs slower through slack water where the bed is silt resting on the clay, sometimes faster through 'riffles' where the bed is gravel. Where heavy flows of water have exposed the clay, water voles have made their burrows. As the river nears its junction with the Thames, its tributary the

Glyme brings down limestone and new chalk-loving plants appear on the banks, as do stream water-crowfoot and yellow water lily in the river itself.

Grey wagtails and kingfishers can be seen from its banks, and heron, wild duck and mute swans are common. Out of my study window in Chilson one spring I could see a dozen swans' nests, great shallow saucers of twigs and stalks on the river-bank, and enjoy the pleasure of watching them raise their broods by the spring. Birds are plentiful. With no special knowl-edge we have seen more than a couple of dozen species of birds in our garden, and we can hear both barn and tawny owls most nights. This is not wild land. You have to go north to the Pennines or west to Wales to find anything that could be called wild. The Evenlode flows either through farm land or through woodland, remnants of the once great royal hunting forest of Wychwood. But there are still plenty of animals around.

The forest of Wychwood was organized around the preser-vation of deer for the king's hunting and that of favoured lords. In the eighteenth century a hundred deer a year were killed. By the 1930s, deer were hardly found outside the parks of great estates like those of the dukes of Marlborough at Blenheim and Vernon Watney at Cornbury. Yet now there are probably more roe and fallow deer around us than there were in the heyday of Wychwood forest. It is said that they escaped from gentlemen's parks during the second world war. Now if we drive home from Charlbury railway station through the forest at dusk, we are all but certain to see a deer or a cluster of them. I have seen half a dozen on the road just outside Ascott village. Once I counted thirteen jumping the hedge in front of me on the road from Leafield to Finstock. And on one never-to-be forgotten day we saw a herd of thirty-four at Wilcote. I know exactly how many there were because they moved slowly away, then for some inexplicable reason wheeled and jumped the hedge in front of us, one at a time. For me, deer are one of the great pleasures of West Oxfordshire. I was startled by the vehemence with which a friend in Western Connecticut cursed the deer there. Perhaps the difference is Lyme disease, which is rife and dangerous in the United States. Actually it has been known in Britain since the nineteenth century, but is still comparatively rare. It is increasing because the ticks which carry it are increasing, presumably in line with the growth in the deer population.

In the Middle Ages the kings hunted wolves and wild boar as well as the red, roe and fallow deer. The whole question of the extermination of wolves in Britain is confused and disputed. It seems that the last wolf in England was killed in the reign of Henry VII (1485-1527), the last wolf in Scotland (by the giant MacQueen!) in the mid-eighteenth century, and the last wolf in Ireland in the late-eighteenth century. Wild boar were certainly exterminated by hunting, perhaps as early as the end of the thirteenth century, though there are as many as a couple of thousand wild boar in the wild in Sussex, Devon and Herefordshire; they are escapees from wild boar farms, and are probably breeding in the wild. The noble red deer are all but extinct in Oxfordshire. We do have hundreds of the tiny imported muntjak. Many small mammals are common: stoats, weasels, grey squirrels, hares and rabbits galore, shy, nocturnal badgers, otters and voles along the river itself, both returning from the brink of extinction, and foxes, barking and howling in the night.

The Environment Agency's official maps show five streams coming together to form the Evenlode. The most glamorous of these tributary brooks flows through the gardens of a great country house, Sezincote, now like so many such places inhabited by a family of bankers, the Peakes, and before them by the Dugdale family. It was built at the very beginning of the nineteenth century for Sir Charles Cockerell, who had made a fortune in Bengal in the service of the East India Company. The architect was Cockerell's brother, Samuel Pepys Cockerell. This was his first essay in what might be called an Anglo-Mughal style. The main house is crowned by a green

Above: Our tiny river starts its journey between the upraised trunks of twin elephants. Left: Thomas Daniell designed this 'Indian' bridge over one of the streams that are the source of the Evenlode in the gardens of Sezincote, near Moreton-in-Marsh.

copper onion-shaped dome and flanked by a long, curving, colonnaded orangerie, placed so as to make the most of the northern sun. Cockerell was helped by Thomas Daniell, an artist whose Indian prints are still in demand in India as well as in Britain. It was Daniell who designed an Indian bridge over this one of the Evenlode's tributaries, ornamented with bronze Brahmin bulls, and probably Daniell, too, who drew the plans for an Indian shrine in a 'temple pool'. The formal garden at the side of the house is approached between two bronze elephants, their trunks upraised. The Prince Regent, later George IV, taken to see the house, asked Cockerell to do something similar in the oriental manner for him. The result was the Brighton Pavilion.

Other humbler streams west of Moreton-in-Marsh gather together. North of the eponymous village of Evenlode our river is still narrow enough to jump across, almost — if you are young and supple enough — to step across. The moment when they come together and form the Evenlode is arbitrary. But by the time the united stream dashes past the tower of St. Edward's church in Evenlode village and pelts under the straight road from Broadwell, it is no longer a brook, but a vigorous young river, curving through horseshoes in the grass-lands like a miniature Mississippi.

For years we have enjoyed walking along the Oxfordshire Way, which in its middle course along the Evenlode splits in two, so that you can walk on either bank of the river. We first met it when we lived in Chastleton, a few miles south of Moreton-in-Marsh. When we lived in Chilson in the eighties, we could turn out of the village street into School Lane, and pass the old school, then inhabited by an amiable African-

American airman from the base at Upper Heyford and his English girlfriend. (The Upper Heyford base has been closed now and is the site of an ambitious real estate development.) He was popular with the children because, when the village was snowed in, his rusty old Buick and the farm tractor were the only two vehicles with powerful enough engines to get up the slope to the main road. Our children rode into primary school in Charlbury that week on a farm tractor.

If we wanted a circular walk we would cross three fields into Ascott Doyley, named for Robert D'Oilly, son of one of William the Conqueror's tenants-in-chief, who built Oxford castle and another in his manor of Ascott. Then we would double back to the right, cross a railway bridge and pass the noisy dogs at Ascott mill. A plank bridge crosses the

The stripling stream at the village of Evenlode.

11

The Evenlode as it flows through the grounds of Bruern Abbey.

Evenlode. We would end up in a little over a mile at Pudlicote, where the manor house was inhabited by another wealthy Londoner, this time a Lloyd's broker, who kept horses in the meadow between his house and the river. Then we would cross another ancient stone bridge and back into our village. Once that last lap of our circuit would have been sheltered by ancient elms, but the elms disappeared in the 1970s. The American construction brigades (Sea Bees) used to say 'the impossible takes a little longer'. You might say 'the immemorial lasts a little longer'.

Some time after we moved back from Oxford to Finstock, I formed the project of walking the whole length of the

Evenlode in comfortable stages of four or five miles at a time, which — if we were to do it by circular walks with a single car — implied a couple of miles of progress each weekend when the weather was acceptable. Usually Hilary and I would set out together. Sometimes my son Francis, doughty walker, two metres tall with a stride to match, would join us. Latterly he would be somewhat slowed down by the weight of his small son Angus, sitting on his shoulders.

First, of course, we went in search of the source of the Evenlode. There was no monument to mark it, like the bearded stone figure at Thames Head near Cirencester, or the baroque pomposity of the basin in the prince's park at Donaueschingen. We ate our sandwiches in a field just north of Evenlode village and headed north through a wood. Eventually we reached a cart track that crossed both the stripling stream and the Cotswold Line railway, before turning south to make it a circular walk. Here the Evenlode Valley is a shallow bowl of rich arable land and woodland with many big oaks along the lines of the hedgerows. At the point where we turned, only a short way from the conjunction of the contributory streams, we could see the spire of Moreton church, no more than half a mile to our eastward.

South of Evenlode lie the estate and village of Adlestrop. The house is an early example of what is called Strawberry Hill Gothic, and it looks out over a cricket field and a much fished lake. It belonged to Jane Austen's cousin Thomas Leigh, and she is known to have visited three times. Cousin Thomas was a wealthy man and he commissioned Humphrey Repton, the most fashionable landscape gardener in an age crazy about landscape, to lay out the grounds, including the lake. Later he inherited an even more aristocratic property, Stoneleigh Abbey in Warwickshire, where the film of *Jane Eyre* was shot. Stoneleigh impressed Jane's mother as only a palace owned by a cousin would impress a poor rector's wife intent on her family's upward mobility.

The Evenlode Valley is not as popular with film-makers as Death Valley, California. But Kevin Brownlow shot some of his film *Winstanley*, about the seventeenth-century proto-communists, the Diggers, in and around Chastleton House, and once I was working in my study there when I heard a loud noise. I walked across the lane, climbed the bank and peered over the wall. I found myself staring into the lens of a 70 mm Mitchell camera at the moment when Beryl Reid, in eighteenth-century gear for a production of Fielding's *Joseph Andrews*, was declaiming in her incomparable insinuating contralto the immortal line: 'The only thing that moves around here is the horses' bowels!'

The village of Adlestrop is more famous for something else: the poem written by Edward Thomas, who lived at Dymock, near Newent in the Forest of Dean in north-west Gloucestershire. A group of 'Dymock poets', including Lascelles Abercrombie and John Drinkwater, were living there before the first world war, and they were joined by the great American poet, Robert Frost, in early 1914. Edward Thomas, son of a civil servant, who had been struggling to make a living as a freelance writer since he went down from Oxford, moved in next door to the Frosts and they became close friends. The two men used to go for long walks in the surrounding coun-

The river at Adlestrop.

14

tryside. On June 23, 1914, Thomas wrote in one of his field notebooks about his train journey:

> Then we stopped at Adlestrop, thro the willows cd be heard a chain of blackbirds songs at 12.45 & one thrush & no man seen, only a hiss of engine letting off steam. ... Stopping outside Campden by banks of long grass willow herb & meadowsweet, extraordinary silence between the two periods of travel.

There is a glimpse here of the creative process: two raw observations from two different places, at least a year old, cooked into what reads like fresh experience. Several well-known poets, including Frost and Walter de la Mare, had already tried to talk Thomas into writing poetry, but it wasn't until December 1914, as he was hesitating whether to join the army or to move to New England with the Frosts, that he took their advice and wrote his first poem. In July 1915, just over a year after the epiphany that inspired him to write

The sign from the disused station at Adlestrop adorns the bus stop in the village. Inside, the text of the poem, studied by so many for A levels, is preserved.

'Adlestrop', he made up his mind to volunteer. In the short time between December 1914 and January 1917, when he went to France, Thomas wrote 143 poems. He was so unsure of his own talent that the poems published during his lifetime were published under the pseudonym Edward Eastaway. Thomas became an officer and served in the 'garrison' artillery, firing heavy guns. He was killed by blast from a German shell on Easter Monday, April 9, 1917. 'Adlestrop' is his most famous and favourite poem.

> Yes, I remember Adlestrop
> The name because one afternoon
> Of heat the express-train drew up there
> Unwontedly. It was late June.
>
> The steam hiss'd. Some one clear'd his throat.
> No one left and no one came
> On the bare platform. What I saw
> Was Adlestrop — only the name
>
> And willows, willow herb, and grass,
> And meadowsweet, and haycocks dry,
> No wit less still and lonely fair
> Than the high cloudlets in the sky.
>
> And for that minute a blackbird sang
> Close by, and round him, mistier,
> Farther and farther, all the birds
> Of Oxfordshire and Gloucestershire.

The station is disused now, and the old station sign — 'only the name' — has been moved to a literary bus shelter in the village where the text, learned by so many aspirants to A levels, is preserved. The poem is the more poignant if it is remembered that this memory of immemorial peace was vouchsafed a young man wrestling in his own mind whether to expose himself to the hell of war on the Western Front.

John Buchan, who bought the manor house at Elsfield, close enough to Oxford for him to walk into college dinners at Balliol and Brasenose and even walk home after dinner, four miles uphill, worshipped the West Oxfordshire countryside. He worked the forest of Wychwood into historical novels like *Midwinter*, about the dissolution of the monasteries, and *The Blanket of the Dark*, about the 1745 rebellion and the legend that the Young Pretender was hidden at Cornbury. In his 'shockers', as he called them, the best-selling stories about the adventures of a South African mining engineer, Richard Hannay, loosely based on the gigantic British general, 'Tiny' Ironside, Buchan established his hero in a West Oxfordshire manor house, and has him meet his friend Sandy Arbuthnot at a Cotswold inn called The Quiet Woman on the Fosse Way Roman road. Sadly the only establishment of that name today is a rather undistinguished modern café on the outskirts of Chipping Norton.

Buchan was brought up in a Glasgow manse but used to the high hills and sheep farms of the Borders from holidays with a grandfather. He was an undergraduate at Oxford, but it was on a motor tour to Burford during the first world war that he fell in love with the Oxfordshire Cotswolds. In the opening chapter of his best novel, *Mr Standfast*, written about a year after Edward Thomas's train stopped at Adlestrop, Buchan described how his hero has been summoned from commanding a battalion in France to a mysterious meeting by the Secret Service. He starts the journey in a train from Paddington, visits a brother officer who is sadly damaged by shell shock, then is driven to a point close to the manor house where his rendezvous is with a mysterious beauty who whistles the old tune of 'Cherry Ripe'. He elects to walk the last couple of miles over the hills and down through great beechwoods.

'All about him', Buchan wrote, were 'little fields enclosed with walls of grey stone and full of dim sheep'. There are fewer sheep now, many small fields have been opened up for the convenience of combine harvesters, and many of the stone walls have been allowed to crumble away because of the shortage of dry stone wallers. At that moment, Hannay had 'a kind of revelation'. 'I had a vision of what we were fighting for, what we were all fighting for. It was peace, deep and holy and ancient, peace older than the oldest wars, peace which would endure when all our swords were hammered into ploughshares'.

Ninety years and so many wars later, some might dismiss that sentiment as canting chauvinism or Tory propaganda. For me, Buchan caught something of the almost mystical appeal the Cotswold landscape has for so many. Hannay saw a 'stream slipping among its water meadows and could hear the plash of its weir'. Buchan did not say so, but he was describing his feelings about the upper reaches of the Evenlode.

Sadly, the very appeal of the region has turned some off it. The very phrase 'the Cotswolds' conjures up 'deep and holy and ancient peace', but it also conjures up media celebrities, quiz show hosts, City slickers and other plutocratic refugees from London. Smugly, we who live in and around the Evenlode valley believe they infest the southern Cotswolds, round the Prince of Wales's house at Highgrove and other royal residences, more than our less fashionable hills and valleys. Like the French poet, we pride ourselves on our simplicity. We prefer our narrow stream and gentle hills to your Danubes and your Alps. DuBellay liked his little Loir better than the Tiber, and the hill behind his village better than the Palatine mount.

Plus mon Loir gaulois, que le Tibre latin,
Plus mon petit Liré, que le mont Palatin.

In that mood, we congratulate ourselves that our quiet northern part of the Cotswolds is free from royals (though I have myself seen the heir to the throne, out with the Heythrop hunt, at the end of my garden at Chastleton) and, with exceptions noted here, relatively free from media celebrities. Still, nowhere quite symbolizes the high living of new money in the Cotswolds like Daylesford, across the road from Adlestrop park, a mile or two north of Kingham station.

Warren Hastings was new money himself, though he was born in the village and claimed ancient lineage. He was the effective but corrupt governor of Bengal who, accused of walking off with the Begum's diamonds, worth six million pounds in the money of the eighteenth century, replied coolly that he was 'astonished at his own moderation'. After his seven-year trial on impeachment in Westminster Hall, where the managers of the prosecution included the flower of Augustan orators, Edmund Burke, Charles James Fox and Richard Brinsley Sheridan among them, Hastings was acquitted. Brought up to believe he was a descendant of ancient nobility, he had always dreamed of being 'Hastings of

Daylesford'. (There is another link with Jane Austen here: there is reason to believe that Austen's cousin Eliza, who married a bogus French count, was in fact Hastings's natural daughter.[3]) Though his fortune had been much eroded during the trial, enough was left for him to fulfil his dream. He built himself a palace, which in recent years was inhabited by Lord Rothermere, proprietor of the *Daily Mail*, and for a while his wife Ann, later married to Ian Fleming. Then it was bought by the Baron Thyssen, scion of German heavy industry and owner of a fabulous collection of paintings. When the British government refused to agree to his conditions for leaving his pictures to the National Gallery, he took them off to Spain.

Daylesford was bought by Lord Bamford, inheritor of the JCB earth-moving concern, whose wife is committed to mental health as assured by organic food. In what was once the Daylesford home farm, a mile north of Kingham village, she set up what can only be called the most ambitious deli in Europe. The home farm has been elegantly redesigned by an American, Randall Anderson, who previously worked as gardener for Lord Saye and Sele at Broughton Castle, near Banbury. At Daylesford, highly-trained staff, shipped in from London and indeed from abroad, and housed in the barns, serve award-winning cheeses, bread baked on the premises, vegetables of preternatural glossiness, meat raised on another Bamford estate in Staffordshire and wine from organic producers, also in some cases family owned, in France. While the prices for the excellent sourdough bread and the prize-winning cheeses made on the premises are more or less within bounds, items from the *batterie de cuisine* draw a chastened whistle even from well-heeled weekenders as they confront a

21

The Daylesford farm shop brings a rare touch of metropolitan chic to the valley, a mile north of Kingham.

stone pestle and mortar of modest size priced at £400. Beyond this temple to the cult of organic growing and healthy eating Lady Bamford presides over a garden shop for the fastidious, and a couturier where her own cool designs are on offer. All are equally welcome, but Daylesford is no ordinary farm shop: at least one woman drives down from Leeds to do her weekly food shop there, and another woman was heard to tell her friend she was buying a tempting, though no doubt organic, snack to eat on the way home in the helicopter.

❧ FOUR ❧

THIS is the supposedly unchanging England beloved of retired colonials, and celebrated by John Major, the England of village cricket, the Church of England, the Women's Institute, and Elgar at the Three Choirs Festival. Needless to say, this dream does not long survive contact with a complex and in some respects disillusioning reality.

It is easy, when looking at a river like the Evenlode, bubbling its way through a quiet countryside, to suppose that the river too has changed little over the centuries. Its supposedly immemorial charm has attracted poets like Hilaire Belloc:

> The tender Evenlode that makes
> Her meadows hush to hear the sound
> Of waters mingling in the brakes,
> And binds my heart to English ground.
>
> A lovely river, all alone,
> She lingers in the hills and holds
> A hundred little towns of stone,
> Forgotten in the western wolds.

As the judge, Sir Ranulf Crew, put it so sonorously, if sententiously, in his summing-up in the Vere peerage case in 1625, even the most ancient pillars of our past crumble in the end.

> Where is Bohun? Where is Mowbray? Where is Mortimer?
> Nay, which is more and most of all, where is Plantagenet?
> They are entombed in the urns and sepulchres of mortality!

In nature, everything changes, even 'nature'. The English landscape has no immunity from that law. The watermills

23

along the Evenlode have all now stopped clacking, and over the centuries the Evenlode landscape has changed beyond recognition.

What few people realize is how much of that change has taken place in living memory. The character, indeed the very life of the river itself has been dramatically changed by comparatively recent activity. After World War II, various public bodies undertook extensive dredging. The idea, at a time when government was desperate to make Britain more nearly self-sufficient in food, was to eliminate flooding. Before that time, the bed of the Evenlode was semi-circular in section. The rainfall on the westward-facing hills above Cheltenham and on the high Cotswolds generally is significantly heavier than in the Thames Valley. At times of heavy rain in the hills upstream, the river would flood extensively. The river was dredged so that its bed was wider, and more nearly square in section; it is roughly the shape of a square bucket. Where in a natural river slow-moving reaches would alternate with fast-flowing 'riffles', since the dredging the Evenlode's course is 'flashy'.

Belloc called the Evenlode 'tender', and that is how it usually is. In July this year we learned that its mood is not always gentle. I was driving back from Oxford, normally a pleasant but humdrum journey of half an hour. It began to rain as I have never seen it do in this country. The French say it rains 'cords', but these were cables, hawsers; we speak of cats and dogs, but these were tigers and grizzlies.

At Wilcote, I was turned back by the landlord, demonstrating officer-like qualities. The steep dip down to Hunt's Copse, where a friend has his workshop, was full of water. I turned and drove past Holly Grove. In the outskirts of Ramsden, an American lady approached the car and warned me not even to try to get into the village. I took the other fork, to Delly End, and now the rain had shifted gear, from a cloudburst to a monsoon, a phenomenon. Springs sprouted from bloated aquifers, bubbling through the brown torrent that was the lane. I reached the main road from Witney to Charlbury, and turned for home, only to find the road blocked again just past the Bird in Hand. I eventually persuaded a lady in a four-by-four to try the water so that I could follow her, watching her wheels to see whether the flood would be too high for me.

I had to be in Oxford at nine the next morning. I had a sleepless night working out a route high enough to be clear of the water. It would have to be the Charlbury way and I would have to hope the Glyme had not flooded in Woodstock. I had forgotten that between our village and Charlbury the road goes down a long incline to Fawler mill, where it crosses first

In July 2007 Charlbury's cricket field was flooded. The force of the water knocked the coping from the bridge into the river.

the railway, then the river. A Mercedes was heading back, its lights on to warn me. I rounded the corner. A truck was abandoned in the floodwater. A raging, leaping wall of brown water, spurting across the road, made it unthinkable to go on.

This was the 'tender Evenlode", now elemental. In hours, two months' average rainfall had ripped from the sky. Two miles upstream, it had smashed its way through the parapet of a stone bridge by Charlbury station. A car was under water there, almost to the roof, within minutes. Here, at Fawler mill, it had drowned the mill house and pulverized a two foot thick stone wall. It was like seeing an old friend, trusted and reliable, converted overnight into a berserker. An old Latin tag, dimly remembered from schooldays, ran through my head: 'You may drive nature out with a pitchfork, it will always come back".

Three inches of rain fell in as many hours. At the bottom of Pound Hill two cars were under water but no one was drowned.

26

To slow the river down, the Environment Agency, which has taken over responsibility for British rivers from the National Rivers Authority, has carried out an ambitious project. For about a mile, just above the point where the river Glyme joins the Evenlode at the southern end of the duke of Marlborough's Blenheim Park, between Long Hanborough and Bladon, the agency has deliberately introduced artificial meanders by tipping gravel on alternate sides of the water-course. It has also created a small new backwater, to encourage fish and other creatures to breed. The project, finished in 2006, slows the stream, and it is anticipated that this will help all forms of wildlife, from weed through invertebrates to mammals. By the 1970s, as a result of pollution by fertilizers and pesticides, several mammals were coming close to extinction in the river, as in other lowland rivers of southern England. In recent years, however, several of these species have re-established themselves in the Cotswold rivers. Otters have certainly returned to residence and are found throughout the Evenlode catchment area.

≋ FIVE ≋

THE far-reaching consequences of something almost unnoticed even by those who live along the Evenlode's banks is a warning against too quick and facile a sentimentality about our landscape. I love the Evenlode valley, which is why I have chosen to live there three times: in Chastleton, in Chilson and in Finstock. But I don't want my feeling for it to melt into an escapist Englishry, like the sentimentality of some of the 'Sussex-by-the-Sea' Georgian poets. Like many of us, I appreciate the apparently unchanging character of our West Oxfordshire environment. But I also notice that underneath that appearance of immobility, it changes, changes fast, and certainly not always equally for the good of everyone who lives there. There has been, for example, a good deal of discussion, angry or anguished, about the effect of in-migration on the price of houses, with the result that many young people cannot afford to live in places where their families lived for decades, or even for centuries. This is only one example of a whole interlocking network of problems for rural societies abruptly challenged by rapid change, in part precisely because they are seen by city people as innocent as well as idyllic. But the issues are more complicated than they seem.

Our poetic memory of a Golden Age of prosperous agricultural tranquillity is reinforced by dozens of writers, but also by a growing and powerful tourism industry for which the golden vision of the Cotswolds past is nothing more or less than stock-in-trade. I do not need to labour the point that the rural past was neither happy, nor untroubled, nor unchanging. Thomas Gray was right. The annals of the rural poor were 'short and simple'. Their lives were also frightening, dangerous and painful. They were threatened by disease unattended by medical care, the constant fear of hunger, and the real danger of often savage punishments. And even if catastrophe was avoided, the unavoidable experience for the great majority of both men and women was hard, exhausting physical work.

I see this most clearly through the example of the Evenlode valley hamlet where we lived from 1978 to 1983. Chilson is a

28

very ancient settlement, almost certainly Roman and probably older than that. In the early twentieth century, as it had been for several centuries, it was a place wholly occupied with farming land held on a tenancy from the Cornbury estate. When we lived there, Chilson had about 70 inhabitants and thirty dwellings. In 1900 one of those houses was lived in by a farmer who rented about six hundred acres from Cornbury. The rest of those thirty-odd houses and cottages were inhabited by men who worked for the farm as labourers or as specialist 'horse chaps', ploughmen or shepherds.

By the time we arrived to live there in 1978, the farm was still owned by Cornbury, and the tenant, Michael Badger, had invested massive capital in tractors, combines, grain-drying equipment and other machinery, so that the farm could be run by himself, his son and one hired man. I do not have the figures to prove it, but I do not doubt that these three men produced many times more in real terms than the thirty men who lived there in 1900.

Where had the thirty men of Chilson gone? Some no doubt were killed in the first world war. I do not know how many, because Chilson, unlike most Evenlode valley villages, does not have a war memorial. It does not have a church of its own. Church people walked to lovely Shorthampton church, half a mile away. There was a Methodist chapel in Chilson, and even in our day there were 'camp meetings', with deep-throated hymn singing accompanied by the Stonesfield silver band. Much of West Oxfordshire was chapel country.

After the 1918 armistice, men looked for work elsewhere, and their families followed them. Perhaps some emigrated to Canada or Australia. Many of the numerous Pratley clan had already settled in New Zealand. Others moved into English towns. One of the largest single destinations was the Morris Motors car factory at Cowley in East Oxford, which was hiring thousands of workers in the 1920s and again in the brief boom of 'new' industries in the late 1930s. Many of those who grew up in Chilson moved into the new council house estates in Cowley, and some bought bungalows in developments like Farmoor and Bablockhythe, putting a foot on the famous property ladder.

Notionally, some two dozen pretty stone houses or cottages in Chilson must have been left untenanted by the operation of economic laws, that is by the entirely rational search on the part of the former agricultural labourers of Chilson and their children for an easier and better life. What ought to have happened to those houses? In earlier centuries, when hundreds of thousands (including my forebears from Swaledale) left the upland villages of the Pennines and crowded into Leeds, Bradford and Manchester, those villages mostly crumbled away: you can sometimes see their traces in the Yorkshire Dales, the Peak or North Lancashire. But Chilson and the other villages of West Oxfordshire lost most of their agricultural population, not in the railway age, but in the age of the motor car. Railways, as a rule, concentrate, cars disperse.

The result was that other inhabitants, including us, moved in and did what they could, within the constraints of their means and of the planning laws, to convert what had once been the labourers' cottages of Chilson into a dream of rural peace and beauty. We bought our house from a law lecturer, who was also an artist, at a university in the Midlands. Some of these people were retired. One was a

A glimpse of Chilson with the dark fleece of Wychwood on the opposite hill.

learned professor of Egyptology from Oxford University, son of a famous composer, who had taught himself Japanese in the national interest to do intelligence work in world war II. Another was an accountant who had owned a smart restaurant in West London. Most had jobs in Oxford or Witney. Some worked elsewhere: one was an officer in the R.A.F., another a sales executive with a food company. Some of us worked in London. I was a freelance journalist at the time. I wrote a book about the American presidency, and went up to London by train and presented the London Programme on television every week, and spent two or three nights a week in our flat in Bloomsbury. Francis Sitwell, our neighbour and great friend across the street in Chilson, worked in a City public relations firm and came down with his family only at weekends and in the summer, like the 'summer people' of northern New England. Another neighbour, a woman, was the head of the fire service in Cambridge and commuted by car to work there. Later the linguist's cottage was bought as a retirement home by a very senior civil servant. There were also people, almost all of them retired and mostly elderly, who had grown up in Chilson. A quarter of a century later, almost none are left.

The obvious point, and it was true, is that we 'incomers' had pushed up the price of houses in Chilson, hardly to dizzy heights, but certainly to the point where most of the young people who had grown up there, starting out in life with young families, could not afford them. That was a destructive effect, but it is not easy to see how it can be avoided, short of unacceptable interference in personal freedom. The less obvious point was that the economic system, the famous 'market', had worked, not indeed without victims, but nevertheless as it is supposed to work. Most of five or six dozen people were organizing themselves to live in Chilson because they wanted to live there, and because the wealth and complexity of a modern post-industrial society made it possible for them to have the best of two or more worlds. The same is true of the Evenlode valley, from Moreton-in-Marsh to the outskirts of Oxford, indeed of West Oxfordshire as a whole, and for that matter of much of rural England. When I went to interview the leader of the rebellion against the management of Lloyds of London, I found him in Kingham, and our new home, Finstock, has been home to a well-known novelist, an actor, two motor-racing engineers, the manager of a London opera company, and many people working in new technologies.

This transformation, of course, is far from free of problems. A village, to survive as what the planners call a 'sustainable' settlement, needs to have a primary school, a shop, as well as a church and at least one pub. Our village lost its shop, but we have clubbed together to start a new one, with the help of substantial grants available for this purpose from central and local government, and the same has happened in Kingham, Ascott and other villages along the Evenlode valley. We still have an excellent primary school, but as the average age in the village rises, enrolment falls, and the long-term survival of the school becomes problematic. But social change is so vast, its causes so deep in the past, and so far-flung in space, that it can neither be stopped or avoided. It is one small example of the titanic working out of economic and social processes that date back to the nineteenth century. These include, and the list is far from exclusive, the loss of captive markets for Britain's heavy industry; the Victorian Tory strategy of replacing British agriculture with cheap food from the Empire and the United States; the love of the countryside and the imagined past that were both Victorian responses to the dark satanic mills and disconcerting change of the industrial revolution; and of course two world wars and the loss of empire. The consequence has been that if you drive through Chilson, or any of Hilaire Belloc's 'hundred little towns of stone', you could easily suppose them unchanging. But you would be wrong. In reality they have arguably changed more rapidly and radically, for better and for worse, in the past thirty years than in the previous three hundred.

⪻ SIX ⪼

IN 2005 Kingham had the (perhaps dangerous) distinction of being named by *Country Life* as the most desirable village in England. It is certainly attractive. Its stone houses are attractively group round a traditional village green. It has a church, a handsome rectory (inhabited for a while by an American insurance executive), and several other substantial homes. It has an excellent primary school, a thriving village shop, a restaurant, a football team, a British Legion club and many other village activities. It was the home of two great Victorians. One was the Oxford classics don and naturalist, William Warde Fowler, who used to invite his students to 'reading parties' in Kingham and died in 1921. The other was the eccentric benefactor of poor children, Charles Baring Young. He built the Kingham Homes for slum boys a mile or so from the village, now Kingham Hill School, and endowed it more generously than anyone who saw him in his shabby coat and frayed trousers could have believed.

Kingham station, too, has its character. Across the permanent way is the Langston Arms where, when we lived at Chastleton, I used to wait for trains in the hotel bar. Mac, a richly bewhiskered Scot who ran horse and carriage tours of the Cotswolds from the inn's stables, used to come into the bar in vaguely military waterproof gear and a deerstalker cap and invariably ask: 'All sigarny?' When he had gone, we would argue about the derivation of this saying. Some said it was Romany. Others that it was short for 'All Sir Garnett?' – a reference to Sir Garnett Wolsey, field marshal and commander-in-chief in Boer War days, and a legendary stickler for 'good order and military discipline'. The hotel commemorates Squire James Langston of Sarsden, owner of some ten thousand acres in the flush times before the repeal of the Corn Laws. The stables at the Langston Arms have now been converted into business units, one of which produces a fine goat's cheese.

Langston was a great patron of building and architecture. He employed the Oxford architect, James Plowman, to build a scale model of Magdalen College tower for the parish church in Churchill and rebuilt many of his farms. Churchill tower can be seen on the horizon from the Evenlode valley around Kingham. Langston marked the entrance to his ground with stone balls on the high road from Burford to Chipping Norton and he built the elegant town hall in the latter town, opposite the Fox inn where the Heythrop hunt meets. (The irrepressible Tamara Malcolm, founder and presiding genius of the Theatre, Chipping Norton, was rumoured to have borrowed an elephant from Chipperfield's Circus, who winter nearby, to frighten the horses. Tamara denies this, and says she only thought of this original ploy, and never played it.)

The first chapter of our exploration of the river began at the headwaters and took us by stages to a few yards west of Kingham station, where the Evenlode bursts out of the old site of Bledington mill, runs between two buildings and is crossed by the road. We walked south, past Foxholes, where an old lady I met on the train once told me she looked after a house full of some thirty refugee children from all over the world, rather in the manner of Josephine Baker in her chateau overlooking the Dordogne. We explored Bould Wood. This is one of the eighty-eight nature reserves maintained by the admirable Berkshire, Buckinghamshire and Oxfordshire Wildlife Trust. (It likes to be called BBOWT, but is still universally known as BBONT.) It is a peaceful, unspoiled tract of 165 acres of beautiful woodland. In spring it is beloved for its bluebells. In autumn its fungi are spectacular. At all times, it is full of birds.

At the hamlet of Bould, we circled back towards Bledington. The Westcote brook, a small tributary of the Evenlode, runs through the village green, and has caused the villagers to put up signs warning motorists of the village ducks. The village pub, on the green, was once known as Fag-ash Annie's, because the ash from the landlady's cigarette was all too likely to fall into the beer. Now it is an elegant gastropub, run by the Orr-Ewings, and was one of the headquarters of the county's resistance to the parliamentary ban on hunting with dogs. Two millstones leaning against a wall are all that is left of Bledington mill.

Nearby are the two handsome Oddington villages, Upper Oddington and Lower Oddington, with another attractive gastropub, The Fox, and several handsome houses. A short walk takes one to St Nicholas's church. Alongside the lane there is a wood which in spring is carpeted with the tiny white cruciform flowers of wild garlic. In the old church there is a magnificent thirteenth-century 'doom', recently restored. A doom is a Last Judgment. The Oddington villagers could draw their own conclusions as they saw the just being led to a city of delights, while the unjust are hanged on gallows and crammed into huge cooking pots by sadistic-looking devils.

*Looking back towards Bruern Abbey from the ride
through Bruern Wood.*

Another day's walk took us through the Astor estate at
Bruern. To make it a circular walk, we parked by the church
in Shipton, crossed the A361 and walked to Priory farm on
the edge of Lyneham, then crossed the new golf course. Some
of the golfers helped us by kindly showing us the way. Others
bellowed 'Fore!' like boorish caricatures in a 1920s *Punch*. At
Bruern, we crossed the railway and immediately afterwards
the Evenlode and walked past Bruern abbey. The big house
has been sold, but there are still Astors living in several other
houses nearby. Bruern abbey itself was built in the middle of
the twelfth century by the Cistercians, an order of monks who
sought out remote and beautiful places — among them the

Yorkshire Dales, the Welsh marches and Provence — and tended to thrive on the flocks and the mines they could develop away from towns. Bruern after all means 'the briars' (from the French bruyère, Latin briaria). The modern house was built by the Cope family in the eighteenth century and remodelled by the Astors. It had been inhabited in Victorian times by a Portuguese banker who commuted by train to the City of London, forerunner in that respect of the owners of those big Mercedeses at Kingham station. Immediately south of his house, a ride has been cut through the woods aligned with it, so you see the Palladian façade framed through the trees behind you, until you dodge through a hedge, plough through two unusually muddy fields, and find yourself rejoining the Evenlode as you march into Shipton-under-Wychwood.

Sheep safely grazing by the Evenlode at Bruern.

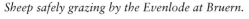

38

Shipton's twin village is Milton-under-Wychwood, another village that is full of life and activity. When we lived in Chilson, our family doctor was young Doctor Scott, whose partner sometimes came to the surgery in hunting boots, breeches and pink coat. Dr Scott's father had the playwright, Christopher Fry as a patient. Fry's verse dramas (*The Lady's Not for Burning*, *Venus Observed*, and the rest, unlikely best-sellers of the postwar years) did not apparently come easily. When his patient came to him for help, Dr Scott would say, 'Well now Mr Fry, what's it going to be this time? Whisky or barbiturates? You can't have both, you know!'

Shipton is a pleasant settlement, grouped round a modern village green. Its village cricket team reached the national finals for teams in their category, though the traditionally peaceful atmosphere of village cricket was shattered by a regrettable incident in which one player went for another with a cricket bat.

One of the stars of Shipton's team was Sam Mendes, who won an Academy Award for directing *American Beauty*. Mendes helped Shipton get into the final of the village championship at Lord's by hitting 48 in just 26 balls. He learned his cricket at Magdalen College School in Oxford, where he was in the XI for three years. In his last year he made 552 runs and took 37 wickets and was chosen to play for The Rest agaist Southern Schools in a trial for the England Schools team.

John Foxe, the author of *Foxe's Monuments*, better known as *Foxe's Book of Martyrs*, prebendary of Salisbury cathedral, spent eleven years as the incumbent of Shipton until he was so emaciated his own friends did not recognize him. He had grown thin meticulously chronicling the sufferings of Christian martyrs from the time of Nero to that of Bloody Mary, with particular reference to the recent torments inflicted on Protestants. It is depressing to think of a man so obsessed with torture and violent death in such idyllic surroundings. But the *Book of Martyrs* became the gruesome bestseller of the sixteenth century, and probably did a great deal, by reminding everyone of the Marian persecution, to ensure that England would remain a Protestant country until the twentieth century.

The prebendal house, where Foxe presumably lived, was extended in the seventeenth century into something resembling the manner of the 'wonder houses' designed by Robert Smithson. The family of Rufus Isaacs, later Lord Reading, the great lawyer and member of the Lloyd George cabinet, lived in Shipton until late in the twentieth century. There is also a modern house, designed by Stout and Lichfield in 1964, with a Japanese water garden described by Sir Nikolaus Pevsner's guide as 'one of the outstanding modern private houses in the country'. The Shaven Crown, a popular pub in the village street, was built in the fourteenth century as a guesthouse of Bruern Abbey, and mediaeval work survives there.

At Shipton, the Evenlode turns to the east and runs between the long ridge that reaches its highest point at Lyneham hill, and the remaining rump of Wychwood, protected from development because it has belonged since the civil war to the Cornbury estate. Some historians believe that Wychwood means the wood of the Hwicce, an Anglo-Saxon people who occupied the land from Oxfordshire across northern Gloucestershire and southern Worcestershire to Herefordshire, where they marched with the embattled Romano-Celts known as the Welsh. Others disagree.

Wychwood from near Catsham bridge over the river on the road from Leafield to Chadlington.

Under the Norman and Angevin kings, with their passion for hunting, Wychwood became a royal forest. That did not mean that it was densely covered with trees, although it is still spotted with 'thousand year old oaks', many of them genuinely at least several centuries old. The forest was a hunting preserve,[4] containing both woodland and rough ground not used for farming. The essential point was that it was subject, not to the common law of England, but to the forest law, by which a man interfering with the king's game or with his sport could be subject to savage penalties, including blinding and castration, though these were almost always commuted for money. Today the Evenlode seems to run round Wychwood, skirting the continuous woodland as it flows from Shipton to Charlbury, and again leaving the ancient forest on its right bank as it turns the corner and

The Cornbury deer, descendants of the king's Wychwood herds.

runs south from Charlbury through the 'gorge' to Hanborough and Eynsham. But once upon a time Wychwood covered all the land between the Thames and the Cherwell, as far west as Burford and as far north as the Sars brook, which runs from near Chipping Norton into the Evenlode just north of Bruern. Over the centuries Wychwood has shrunk, until the only continuous woodland is in the Cornbury estate, though there are still other ancient and extensive woods, like Singe (St John) Wood at Whiteoak Green near Hailey or Eynsham woods, east of Witney between the A40 and the Bladon-Witney road. The Sarsden and Ditchley estates, on the left bank of the river, are a reminder of how far the woodland once stretched.

The history of the forest is complicated. You have to distinguish between the much more extensive royal hunting forest and the much smaller, but still broad royal demesne forests of Woodstock, Cornbury and Wychwood. At various times in history, in the reign of Henry II in the twelfth century and again in the reigns of James I (a keen hunter) and Charles I in the seventeenth, kings and their agents tried to enforce the wider boundary. Charles's effort to do so, not just in Wychwood but in the other royal forests as well, was meant to free himself from the tiresome interference of Parliament, and so was an important contributory cause of the Civil War.

In the Middle Ages, and as late as the time of Sir Henry Lee of Ditchley, favourite of Queen Elizabeth and Ranger of the manor of Woodstock, the forest was full of outlaws. Indeed as late as the nineteenth century Wychwood was notorious as the home of 'poachers, deer stealers, thieves and pilferers of every kind', as the agricultural reformer Arthur Young put it in 1813. 'Oxford gaol would be uninhabited', he added, 'were it not for this fertile source of crime'. Wychwood was finally 'disafforested' in the 1850s. The motive was a typically Victorian impatience with rowdy and unruly behaviour, combined with a desire for economic progress. Disafforestation was essentially the abolition of a legal status. Much of the area remains wooded to this day, and the core of the forest, some 3,000 acres round Cornbury, is solid woodland.

Some of the forest villages, notably Leafield, grew out of the rough settlements of these poachers and footpads. Other villages, like Ramsden, were the home of the guardians of the Forest law, gamekeepers and sworn enemies of the outlaws. To this day, the memories linger of bad blood between the poachers and the gamekeepers who hanged them or chopped off their hands. When we first lived in Chilson in the early 1980s it was still said that if a Leafield girl went out with a boy from Ramsden, she risked being cold-shouldered in the playground. But things change. Now children from all the forest villages are likely to go to secondary school in either Witney or Chipping Norton. Taboos that have lasted for centuries can fade fast.

⇌ SEVEN ⇌

IF YOU LOOK at an Ordnance Survey map of the river, you can easily spot where the mills are, or were, by the double blue line of mill race (to drive the wheel) and mill leet, to carry the rest of the water downstream and control the flow. Domesday Book records mills in 1086 in Cassington, Eynsham, Bladon, Hanborough, Combe, and Ashford, near Wilcote, as well as at Evenlode. Later there were mills at Fawler, Charlbury, Ascott, Shipton, Bledington and at Kingham.

Where in the Derbyshire or Yorkshire Dales or in the Lake District, the mills were quite early used to drive machinery making nails, or bobbins, or other simple industrial machinery, our Evenlode mills were mostly grist mills, used for grinding the flour of what was always, except for the forest, a predominantly agricultural region. In the 1850s flour milling ceased at Combe mill. The duke of Marlborough (whose family had come to own half a dozen mills and had demolished the mill at Bladon in the process of damming the Glyme to make their lake at Blenheim) installed steam machinery (that can still be visited) to make a sawmill, which is still in operation.

Only at Shipton-under-Wychwood is there still a working mill grinding flour, and it is no longer a water mill. The mill building, installed in 1911-12, is still operated by F.W.P. Matthews Ltd. who began as a seed merchant in the 1860s. (It is not to be confused with Shipton Mill, near Tetbury in the southern Cotswolds.) The Matthews mill at Shipton for many years specialized in making soft biscuit flour for Huntley & Palmer in Reading, Jacobs in Dublin and Peek Frean in Bermondsey. In the 1960s the company, which is still run by great-grandsons of the bearded mid-Victorian founder, decided to concentrate on high quality bread flour, mostly organic, largely milled from locally grown wheat.

Good cloth has been made in the Cotswolds for centuries, and the tall chimney of the Bliss tweed mill in Chipping Norton is a reminder that a few textile factories, making West of England cloth, were always to be found within the northern Cotswolds, as well as in the Stroud area with its Golden Valley further south. The Bliss mill is now luxury flats.

In spite of this modest industrial past, the Evenlode has always been essentially agricultural and especially pastoral. It does run through some of the loveliest of quiet English land-scapes, curving sinuously from the high Cotswolds through Wychwood forest to the Thames valley. It is a wonderful river for walkers. There are places where they are kept away from the river bank by buildings, but they are not many. There are places where landowners do not allow walkers along the river. But most of the walks I have described are on the Oxfordshire Way or other rights of way. Sometimes, nettle beds protect the bank itself. But on the whole for most of its length there are pleasant, easy walks on both banks. It is true that these are by no means all rights of way. Between Shipton and Charlbury the Oxfordshire Way runs parallel with the river, and there are other stretches which, while not officially rights of way, are locally popular walks.

It is a good fishing river, with fishing rights for most of its course owned by the Chipping Norton Angling Society, the Charlbury Angling Club and Red Spinners, whose water runs down from Fawler to the Isis fish farm, close to the round-about on the edge of Eynsham. There are plenty of chub, roach and dace on the bottom, for coarse fishermen (that is practitioners of coarse fishing, most of them, no doubt, persons of unimpeachable refinement). The angling clubs keep the river well stocked with coarse fish, though in England anglers normally throw their catch back. Even perch, regarded as a delicacy in the United States as well as in France, are not usually eaten. Barbel are found below the Isis fish farm (the former Eynsham mill), and rudd, tench and bream enter the Evenlode from the Glyme, which swells out to form the great lake in Blenheim park. Pike are quite common in the lower reaches, some of them as big as ten pounds. Three of them were found in one short reach in the course of a fish survey.

Trout are to be seen, nosing through the weed in many places for those who want to fish with the fly. These are native brown trout, not the imported rainbow trout found in commercial fish farms. From Lyneham, near Bruern, they share the river with coarse fish, and they are dominant as far down as Shipton. Even more rich in trout are the tributaries, some of them tiny, such as the Cornwell brook. (Cornwell, now the home of the Ward family, is a gem of a Cotswold manor house. It was rebuilt in the 1930s by Sir Clough Williams-Ellis on the orders of its then American owner as an elegant estate village.) There are plenty of trout in the Sars brook, which marks the ancient northern boundary of Wychwood at its widest extent and flows into the Evenlode just north of Bruern, in the Kingham brook, the Chadlington stream, and in the tiny Coldron brook that runs down through woodland from near Spelsbury into the river just before it reaches Charlbury.

Only at Charlbury railway station — the only one I know, incidentally, from which you can see a herd of deer when they are in a mood to be observed — is the river close to Wychwood, known locally simply as 'the forest'. The string of ponds in the Cornbury estate are managed as fisheries, and empty into the Evenlode below Charlbury station. The river glides in a great curve past the outskirts of the Wychwood villages, Shipton and Ascott, while Stonesfield, Combe and Hanborough sit high above it. Every mile or so it divides to make room for a water mill. From the point of view of fisheries, in fact, the river is split up into a dozen and more distinct sections, each anything from one to four miles long. Fry do drift downstream past mills, but adult fish cannot swim upstream past them or past weirs, so that from a fishery point of view the river is effectively divided into a series of sections.

The small tributaries are the home not only of abundant trout but also more surprisingly of lampreys. These are not,

47

however, the sea-going monsters who make their way from their breeding grounds in the dense weed of the Sargasso sea in the subtropical Atlantic. These were so prized by mediaeval kings that several of them, including our own Bad King John, surfeited on them and died. They are still cooked in a rich sauce of their own blood and copious quantities of claret in the restaurants of Bordeaux. The Evenlode brook lampreys are tiny. As little more than larvae, they live in the silt at the bottom of streams. Briefly, they turn into fish, with a fin, before they die.

The Evenlode is rich in crayfish. But the native white-clawed crayfish, *Austropotamobius pallipes*, has been all but eliminated by an imported North American species, the 'signal crayfish', *Pacifastacus leniusculus*. The story is reminiscent of the relentless replacement of the native red squirrel by the North American grey squirrel. It is complicated by the fact that there are other crayfish varieties involved, including *Astacus astacus*, introduced from Morocco via France, not to mention the Lousiana Red Swamp variety (*Procambarus clarkii*), the hero of many appetizing dishes in the restaurants of the New Orleans French Quarter. But the main event on the Evenlode is the one-sided competition between *Austropotamobius* and *Pacifastacus*.

The story began in Italy as long ago as 1860 when the cray-fish plague first arrived there in ballast water in an American ship and spread gradually through Europe. It reached Sweden in 1907 and was introduced into Britain in crayfish farms in the 1970s, but soon escaped. In most of Britain it has now almost eliminated the native variety. It is no contest. Signals are much bigger and stronger. They are perfectly capable of

48

walking overland to find new sites. They not only have more young, but they breed earlier in the season, so that by the time the native crayfish young appear, the signals are already in command of the site. The unkindest cut is that some signals carry a fungus (*Aphanomyces astaci*) that causes crayfish plague. The signals are usually immune, but the plague kills virtually all infected white-clawed crayfish. There are sinister stories of poachers tipping buckets full of signal crayfish into the river off bridges, then coming back to collect their offspring to sell to restaurants. A bad business!

EIGHT

A FAIR share of English history has taken place near Evenlode's banks, from the Romans' victories over Dobruni and Catevellauni within the broken rectangle of Grimsditch, built by the Celts in the Iron Age, before the Roman settlement, to World War II, when Winston Churchill spent his weekends at Ditchley Park, just two miles from Charlbury. This was then the home of Ronald and Marietta Tree. He was the heir to a Chicago department store fortune. She was later the mistress of Adlai Stevenson, the Democratic candidate for the American presidency in 1952 and 1956. Now Ditchley is a conference centre traditionally with an Anglo-American flavour, though others are often invited now.

Churchill was an Evenlode valley man. He was born at Blenheim Palace and was buried at Bladon, and the Evenlode runs past the first and through the second. Indeed there is a school of thought, which has the authority of *The Place-*

names of Oxfordshire,[5] that the derivation of 'Evenlode', that beautiful word with its two open vowels and its magical hint of evening riches, is nothing more romantic than a corruption of 'Bladon', *bladene* in Anglo-Saxon. The name Evenlode itself, on the same authority, is no more than a 'back-formation' from the village of Evenlode. (When we came to sell our cottage at Chastleton, I was inspired to say that it was in the Evenlode valley. Such was the magic power of the word that although the Sunday newspaper in which I had inserted the ad left out one digit of my telephone number, we still had an offer from a lady novelist by lunchtime.)

Certainly, while the upper reaches have long been called the Evenlode, after the village of that name, there was a time when the lower stretch below Hanborough and Blenheim Park was known as the Bladon stream.

West Oxfordshire, according to recent statistics, is the least populated district in the Home Counties, with only 135 inhabitants per square kilometre. Indeed, once you are past Oxford, you are for the most part in unspoiled country that has more in common with Somerset or Herefordshire than with Bucks or Herts, even if incomers, mostly from London, are steadily buying up the more appetising properties as second homes.

At intervals, though, the currents of national conflict have disturbed even this deeply rural backwater. It was at Stow-on-the-Wold, no more than four miles uphill from Adlestrop Bridge on the Evenlode, that the veteran cavalier

The garden front of Chastleton house. It was here, in 1865, that the rules of the game of croquet, still played here, were first codified.

commander, Sir Marmaduke Aston, surrendered the last of Charles I's armies. Sitting on a drum, he cheerfully warned his Cromwellian captors that 'you have nothing to do now but to fall out among yourselves', and how right he was.

Fifteen years or so later, there is a story that Charles II, fleeing to the south coast after his defeat at Worcester and an uncomfortable night hiding in the Boscobel oak, was sheltered from Cromwell's troopers by the Jones family at Chastleton, on the hill only a mile from Evenlode village. It is much more plausible that it was Arthur Jones himself, the squire of Chastleton, who galloped home from Worcester, just ahead of Cromwell's pursuing soldiers. There is a story that one of the Jones women served laudanum to them in their wine to fuddle their search.

When Charles was restored to the throne, he granted the manor of Cornbury in the heart of Wychwood to his loyal ally Edward Hyde, now created earl of Clarendon, who wrote there his monumental *History of the Great Rebellion*. Charles's boon companion, the priapic poet Lord Rochester, died nearby and is buried in Spelsbury church, which can be seen from the Oxfordshire Way on the north bank of the river. His life and his verses were both utterly scandalous, and until recently strait-laced Anglican vicars have kept his connection with their church quiet, preferring to remember the parish's association with the ancestors of Robert E. Lee, who lived at Ditchley. One bold admirer of the poet, later editor of the *Times Literary Supplement*, has scrawled an indignant note in the visitors' book protesting this injustice to a great, if disreputable, English poet.

Rochester pinned to the king's bedroom door his famous quatrain:

Here lies our sovereign lord the king,
Whose word no man relies on.
He never said a foolish thing
Nor ever did a wise one.

Rochester might have lost his head for his impertinence. Instead, Charles capped his friend's verses: 'True, my lord', was his riposte, 'for my words are my own, but my actions are my ministers!"

❦ NINE ❦

FOR the whole of its course the river is never more than a few hundred yards away from the railway. The last designed by the great Isambard Kingdom Brunel in 1845, it was finished in 1853. It has now been dubbed the Cotswold Line in the hope of attracting tourists, which it does with some success. Various American agencies advertise cycling holidays in the Cotswolds, and there are usually a few robust bikes in the luggage van at the tail end of the Paddington train, often destined to Charlbury and a long steep climb up the Burford road. Once, more prosaically, it was officially called the Oxford, Worcester and Wolverhampton railway. (Every bridge on the line is stencilled in white OWW and its number.) Unofficially, it was known as the Old Worse and Worse; it is a myth that the railways, in some golden age before nationalisation in 1947, were uncritically beloved by their customers.

Wolverhampton, dedicated to engineering in the heart of what is called the Black Country, does not fit with the idyllic image more or less justly attributed to the Cotswolds. There

Charlbury station, designed by the great Isambard Kingdom Brunel and still painted in the Great Western Railway's livery of chocolate and cream.

are few more pastoral lines left in England than this after it leaves Oxford and criss-crosses the Evenlode over and over again as it ticks off a sonorous litany of reassuring, mostly small stations, not to mention 'halts' like Combe and Finstock itself, visited by only a couple of trains each way in the day.

Those of us for whom the Cotswold line is a lifeline to London, Heathrow and the greater world soon learn them off by heart from the announcer at Paddington: Slough, Reading, Didcot, Oxford, Hanborough, Charlbury, Kingham, Moreton-in-Marsh, Honeybourne, Evesham, Pershore, Worcester Shrub Hill, Worcester Foregate Street, Great Malvern, Malvern Link, Colwall, Ledbury and Hereford. There's poetry for you, especially since Cow Honeybourne was changed to Honeybourne. There was a time when some trains curved round to Cwm Bran, at the head of the South Wales coalfield, but that didn't seem quite right, any more than Wolverhampton did.

It is not just local chauvinism that makes me favour Charlbury station, and it is not just the off-chance of seeing the fallow deer in Cornbury park. The station building is unspoiled Victorian vernacular, with traces of the chocolate and cream livery of the old Great Western Railway, and a cast iron stove for cold weather. It was built to the design of the great Brunel. The line reached Charlbury in 1853, and four men died digging the cuttings on that part of the line. There were no earth-moving machines, no JCBs, then. Charlbury remains a friendly station. Schoolboys heading for Oxford mingle on the platform with grandees like Douglas Hurd, former foreign secretary, who lives near Burford, or retired ambassadors who have been setting the world to rights at Ditchley Park. The Leader of Her Majesty's Loyal Opposition, David Cameron, lives at Burford and uses Charlbury station, as did the great Ronnie Barker, who lived at Dean Mill and owned an antique shop in Chipping Norton.

For a long time we were looked after by avuncular John, the stationmaster, a retired bank manager from Chippenham who made us feel like his family. There is a fishpond on one side of the booking office, and on the other a carefully looked-after garden on the platform commemorates Sir Peter Parker, debonair chairman of British Rail, who lived in a handsome house with a mediaeval dovecot next to the church and the ruined Lovell manor house in Minster Lovell.

Roughly halfway between London and Stratford, this is favourite territory for actors. John Hurt lived at Ascott, while Sam Mendes, the director of *American Beauty* and his wife Kate Winslet live near Kingham. The incomparable character actor, Freddie Jones, lived in Charlbury. Freddie likes to tell of his experience working with Federico Fellini in Rome. The great director liked to work with what are known as 'ordinary people'. One of these was utterly unteachable. The director would give him his action cue, Freddie said, and this man would unfailingly either do nothing, or do the wrong thing.

'What do you do when you are not trying to act?' asked the great man with glacial sarcasm.

'I'm a professor of comparative philology at the University of Rome.'

'*Esatto*!' said Fellini, confirming his contempt for intellectuals: 'Exactly'.

Freddie was for years the life and soul of the Saturday lunchtime party at the Bell in Charlbury before he transferred his patronage to the Bull. One of his party tricks was to demonstrate with virtuoso technique how a dozen different kinds of smokers hold a cigarette. Sometimes, if these *tours de force*, with their accompanying libations, had gone on so long that the Saturday roast was endangered, Freddie's wife Jenny would send one of the children to shame him home for lunch by appearing in the doorway and intoning 'Father, dear father, come home with me now!'

The car parks at Charlbury, Kingham and Moreton station are full of flash sports numbers and 'Chelsea tractors', and crystalline are the voices that greet the breadwinner in his City suit off the 7:01 p.m. from Paddington. On the morning train up, whole schools of men with velvet tabs on their collars discuss commodities contracts and the price of hunters until Oxford, where even their confident tones are drowned out by the greater fluency of those academics who are off to town to double their academic salaries with consultancy fees.

The great west Oxfordshire estates, too, now belong not only to Whig grandees and foxhunters, but to the international rich: Astors at Bruern, Willses of Imperial Tobacco at Sandford St. Martin, Prince Bandar bin Sultan, long-serving Saudi ambassador in Washington, and recipient of princely douceurs from Her Majesty's Government, at Glympton, and Wafiq Said, broker of the great Saudi arms purchases of the Thatcher era and maecenas of the Oxford University Business School, nearby. (You can tell the homes of these latter oriental magnificos by the exceptional state of repair of their barns and drystone walls.) Sarsden, with its wood-encircled lake, once the home of Flemings, heirs to the inventors of the mutual fund and kinsfolk of the creator of James Bond, now belongs to Shaun Woodward, the Tory member of parliament who crossed the floor to join Labour and is married to a Sainsbury. There is after all nothing incongruous about the presence of these grandees in an alluring stretch of rustic England. They too are part of the pattern of Thatcher's and Blair's neo-England, and they follow the ancient tradition of new money finding security and dignity in country estates, a tradition that goes back, past Lancashire millowners and West Indian slavers, to the great Elizabethan lawyer Coke, handing his fees at the courtroom door to a servant to spur down into Norfolk and buy yet more land, and indeed to the hard men of Henry VIII's reign, speculating in monastic lands.

In the Middle Ages, and as late as the time of Sir Henry Lee of Ditchley, favourite of Queen Elizabeth and Ranger of the manor of Woodstock, the forest was full of outlaws. Some of the forest villages, notably Leafield, grew out of the rough settlements of these poachers and footpads. Witney has been famous for centuries for the Witney Feast. By the late eighteenth century, however, the Feast had become so riotous — the word debauchery was used — that a number of the district's respectable Wesleyan Methodist families, including the Earlys, famous for their blanket works, the Pains of Fawler mill and the Boltons of Finstock, decided to hold a decorous family picnic in the verdant glades of the forest instead. It did not take long, however, before this 'Wychwood Fair', too, had become an event at which no Methodist matriarch would wish her family to be seen. In September 1807 *Jackson's Oxford Journal* reported that 10,000 people had shown up to take part in 'nocturnal orgies'. Showmen and their hurdy-gurdys made the night hideous, and ladies of easy virtue helped themselves to gentlemen's watches. By the 1850s, after the railway had arrived, special trains were run from Oxford for the Fair. Lord Churchill, whose sylvan peace at Cornbury was disturbed and whose sense of proprieties was shocked by the Fair, finally got it closed down after the Forest was finally 'disafforested' by act of parliament in 1857.

≈ TEN ≈

THERE are two places close to the Evenlode where you can still get a sense of the brooding presence of the forest. One is from Chadlington, where the forest appears as a dark fleece thrown over the hills to the opposite side of the Evenlode valley. The other is from just north of Leafield, whose Victorian church spire, designed by Alfred Waterhouse, can be seen from high points all over the forest. As you pass the engineering research centre, once the Post Office's wireless link for transatlantic calls, and pass the equestrian centre run by U.K. Chasers at Crown farm, you get a glorious view of the Evenlode valley swinging like a broad S between gently rounded hills as it curves round the shoulder of Lyneham hill and leads on to Charlbury. Each of the viewpoints over the valley gives it a different character. It has always reminded me, who spent part of my childhood near Pateley Bridge in north Yorkshire, of the soft swelling ridges of the Dales, another landscape of sheep and dry stone walls. Further downstream, in what is somewhat grandiloquently called the Evenlode Gorge, near Combe and Stonesfield, the valley is more deeply incised, more winding and more intimately welcoming, but the view from just below East End, looking across to Combe, and the view southwards from Stonesfield Common towards the Roman villa, are both enticing.

A chain of villages perches on the terraces carved by geological erosion, and Brunel's OWW railway follows the Evenlode as closely as its windings allow. (The ice age glaciers, it seems, only reached as far as the area round Shipton.) From the top of Lyneham hill you look over the Evenlode valley in two directions. To the south you look over Wychwood and in the distance you can see both the Didcot power station a dozen miles south of Oxford and the great white block of the John Radcliffe hospital on the outskirts of the city. To the north, you can see the distant ridge of the Cotswolds beyond Stow, with the old R.A.F. Central Flying School at Rissington and the radio tower on Wyck Hill above Icomb.

When we set out to walk the section of the valley that you glimpse from the hill above Leafield, the next stage of our walk took us to Ascott-under-Wychwood. To find the footpath, you have to walk hazardously along the main road for a quarter of a mile or so in the direction of Chipping Norton, with traffic that has worked up speed coming down the long incline from Lyneham Hill, past seven clumps of beech. That is the tallest hill in the area, with an Iron Age fort and a prehistoric grave site on its summit.

With relief, after dodging the traffic, you cut off the road into a small farmyard on the right, but here you can easily go wrong. If you follow the well-marked path straight ahead, it takes you to a pleasing footbridge which leads into a meadow with tall grass and wildflowers, enclosed by hedges with big forest trees at intervals. But this path leads nowhere, or at best to the metalled road from Shipton to Ascott. (Along this road, incidentally, are some of the few remaining small fields that were normal before the recent process of enlarging fields for combine harvesting.) What you should have done was to turn sharp left, almost parallel with the Chipping Norton road, then climb a stile and follow a hedge on the right through a

The bridge you cross as you enter Ascott Earl,
a good spot for poohsticks.

field of rapeseed. At the end, above a bend in the Evenlode, you cross a little bridge over a ditch and come into a delightful path, with the railway close on your left. This path takes you through a plantation of young trees, and eventually over another bridge, crossing the Evenlode itself, a good place to play poohsticks, into Ascott Earl.

Ascott is still divided into two villages, Ascott Earl, given by William the Conqueror to one of his tenants-in-chief, the earl of Gloucester, and Ascott Doyley, where another, Robert D'Oilly, who built Oxford castle, built a rude earthwork topped with a wooden paling. His family built a square tower with stone curtain walls in Ascott a hundred years later.

Ascott is famous for another set of 'martyrs' from John Foxe's. They are commemorated on a circular bench surrounding a tree in the village green. Their surnames were Moss, Honeybourne and Pratley, and Pratley, at least, is still a common name in West Oxfordshire, even though after the affair many Pratleys emigrated to New Zealand. (Our next-door neighbour, who built our house, is David Pratley, and we get our milk from what used to be Pratley's dairy in Charlbury until it was bought out by Dairy Crest.)

The Ascott martyrs were Victorian housewives, and they were not stretched on the rack or torn with hot irons. They were however sent to prison in Oxford in 1873 because they had gone to work to replace their husbands, early members of Joseph Arch's agricultural workers' union. Victorian values were troubled, even shocked, by the affair. Even Queen Victoria herself, no friend to radical agitation, was sufficiently sympathetic to send the women red flannel petticoats and five shillings apiece, and they were released after inside of a week.

The trouble started when Robert Hambidge of Crown Farm, Ascott sacked his men because they had joined the Agricultural Workers' Union, and then employed men from Ramsden to do his hoeing. (Ever since the days of the Forest Law Ramsden was the village whose inhabitants were on the side of the law, where the other forest villages were the home of poachers and outlaws.) The Ascott women stopped these men from working, and tried to persuade them to join the union. The women were arrested, taken to Chipping Norton, and charged with obstructing and coercing John Hodgkins and John Millen with a view to inducing them to leave their employment. The magistrates, both clergymen, were reluctant to proceed, because they knew they had no alternative but to sentence the women to hard labour. The farmer, however, was adamant. To modern sensibilities an unattractive aspect of the affair is that the Duke of Marlborough, who as the owner of thousands of acres in west Oxfordshire had every interest in keeping out the union, and who was Hambidge's landlord, was also chairman of the bench of magistrates. At any rate, in spite of a riot by 3,000 people outside the court in Chipping Norton, the sixteen women were duly convicted and sentenced, some to ten days' hard labour, and some to seven. They were transported in drays to Oxford prison, some with small children.

Ascott Doyley is essentially one long village street. At the end, you take a lane, cross the railway and brave the noisy dogs in the farmyard of Ascott mill, now a B & B. At this point you are on the island between the mill race and the mill leet. On your left there is a little plank bridge. We have a snap of a big crow sitting on the handrail, daring us to cross. Over the bridge, your best bet is to follow the windings of the Evenlode. This is a classic reach, with water-crowfoot and other weed in the stream and willows on the bank. There is rosebay willow herb, which Americans call fireweed, and Oxfordshire ragwort, poisonous to horses, and anglers sit quietly where they can find a space between the banks of nettles. There are plenty of brown trout nosing their way between the streamers of weed, but between Shipton and Charlbury they are joined by coarse fish, especially chub.

After a couple of fields you have to turn left along a hedge to rejoin the Oxfordshire way, which runs across a field full of horses and their training jumps, under the windows of Pudlicote House, where the track crosses the Chilson road, lined with willows and once, before the Dutch elm disease of

the 1970s, an avenue of giant elms. Pudlicote is now no more than a hamlet, and its only brush with history came in the thirteenth century when a certain John of Pudlicote tried to steal the crown jewels and was flayed alive for his trouble. Now the field is full of hunters and the cavaletti, little jumps, for the Pudlicote children to urge them over.

Pudlicote bridge is one of the places where the river seems at its most typical: narrow, shallow and fast-flowing, with pollarded willows at intervals. It swings from bank to bank, with deep overhangs on the outside of the bends. This is a reach beloved of swans, who make their big nests, like saucers of dried plants, straw and twigs, on banks that still flood in spring in spite of the dredging. Beyond the road, the track continues along the river bank as far as Catsham bridge, which carries the road from Chadlington, half a mile up the hill to the left, into Wychwood.

On this stage, however, the alternative route on the right bank of the Evenlode has the advantage. It bumps up and down hill from Chilson until it reaches another hamlet, Shorthampton, which is no more than a farmhouse, a cluster of cottages and a tiny jewel of a church. It is far too small to boast a tower or a spire. Instead it just has a small pointed belfry. Inside, it is bare and spare, with box pews and a Georgian pulpit. It has a Norman font, and a thirteenth-century arch leads into a tiny chancel added in the nineteenth century. The altar, in true protestant tradition, is a plain oak communion table. There are two eighteenth-century panels, one bearing the Lord's Prayer, the other the Ten Commandments.

Ascott Mill, where a wooden bridge crosses the river.

The only other decoration, on the walls of the nave, are fif-teenth-century paintings. One depicts the miracle described in the apocryphal gospel of Nicodemus. The boy Jesus made birds out of clay and breathed life into them. The Madonna holds the Christ child on one arm, while a boy in green on her other arm and a boy in gold at her feet wonder at a flying golden bird. On another wall is a mediaeval Doom. Miserable sinners are stuffed into the cauldron of hell, to the music of a demon playing the last trump. It is not as wonderful, perhaps, and certainly not as well preserved, as the one in St Nicholas, Oddington, but still a poignant reminder of the eight centuries for which the rude forefathers of this hamlet have worshipped here.

A couple of hundred yards beyond Shorthampton, you have a choice of routes again into Charlbury. You can cross the road and keep to the shorter route a few hundred yards above the south bank of the Evenlode. You will pass the ruins of the manor of Walcot, once the family home of the Jenkinson family, who gave us an obscure prime minister in the early nineteenth century. Then you turn left on to the main Burford to Charlbury road, cross the railway, then the river, and climb Dyer's Hill into Charlbury.

The more rewarding route from Shorthampton to Charlbury, for me, is on the north bank. You have to turn left, cross Catsham Bridge, turn right and walk along a well-marked path, with the river snaking along a field below you to the right. After three fields you go steeply downhill to

The fifteenth-century wall paintings in
Shorthampton church near Chilson.

cross the Chadlington brook. The next half-mile is through land reclaimed and replanted by the Wychwood project, between deep gravel pits protected by signs warning you that the water is deep and dangerous. As you leave the project's land, you reach a lane. Straight ahead you can see Spelsbury church. To the left is a county tip. Beyond it is Dean, inhabited by the City public relations magnate, Lord Chadlington, brother of the former cabinet minister John Selwyn Gummer, and also until recently by David Cameron, Conservative party leader and member of parliament for the Witney division. Next-door is Dean Mill, where Ronnie Barker lived in retirement.

We don't turn left for Dean, however. We turn right to follow the Oxfordshire Way into Charlbury on the left bank of the Evenlode. Further down, beyond some impenetrable woodland full of rusted cars and farm machinery, is Coldron mill, just below Spelsbury church, beautifully converted into a cottage, with a single plank bridge across the millpond. But we don't go that way. Our path runs downhill towards the Evenlode. After the end of the woodland, we cut across a big field full of horses and cows, with plenty of the big horse mushrooms if you're there at the right season and when no one has been there before you. In the far corner of the field a little bridge crosses the Coldron brook, which bellies out to make a miniature pool, full of dragonflies, water boatmen and other assorted pond life. You cross the bridge and pass through a hedge and follow a path through the corn uphill. Then you cross a couple of fields with thorn and scrub to give them a heathland feel, and keep to the edge of a ploughed field, until you find yourself in a hollow lane that

Coldron mill, just below Spelsbury church, beautifully converted into a cottage, with a single plank bridge across the millpond.

leads off to the right. After a couple of hundred yards, you have another choice. You can go left, down a muddy lane that will take you to the point where the road to Spelsbury and Chadlington leaves Charlbury. What we like to do, however, is to turn right. In a few yards you are standing on a weir. This is the head where the race and the leet for Charlbury mill part. The mill was built at least as early as 1363, and lasted until the rural district council demolished it in 1937. Straight ahead are the remains of Walcot, where most of the main house was bought by the duke of Marlborough and pulled down in 1762. But if you turn left after you leave the weir, you have a delightful walk across the mill field between the two branches of the Evenlode.

The weir at the end of Charlbury's Mill Field.

Charlbury church tower from Mill Field

As you approach Charlbury the church tower lies ahead, and on any half-warm evening the river is full of fishermen, children, dogs and picnickers, for this is Charlbury's playground. It was also at one time a religious site, for the Baptist church at the top of Dyer's Hill used the millrace for total immersion as recently as 1914. By the site of the vanished mill, you cross the Evenlode again and reach the main road, turn left up Dyer's Hill, and enter Charlbury.

≈ ELEVEN ≈

THERE is plenty to see in the grey stone metropolis of the Evenlode valley (population an estimated 3,000), and much to love. The heart of the town is Church Street, with handsome stone houses on either side, descending to the twelfth-century church of St. Mary the Virgin, perched above the Evenlode, the railway station and the old trees and deer in Cornbury park, with the forest in the background. At the top of the slope, where Church Street runs into Market Street to the north and Sheep Street to the right, stands the Corner House, once the home of one of Charlbury's two leading families, the Spendloves. It is now a social centre, with the library below and rooms for meetings above. This was rebuilt in elegant style in 1725, complete with a belvedere on the roof, so that for decades it was known as the Observatory. At one time Church Street widened into a Y shape, with the ancient market hall and a market stall covered with a stone slate roof in the space between the two arms. The Market House became a pub and then an ironmonger's, and the roof was finally dismantled in 1871. Lower down is the Albright house, adorned with an ancient wisteria; together with the Spendloves, the Albrights were for centuries the other great Charlbury clan. Lower down on the north side, just before the churchyard, are two houses on the site of what was first known as the Church House, and then

The great wisteria on the front of
Albright House in Church Street, Charlbury.

Church Street, Charlbury. A house first stood where the first house now stands in the twelfth century. Later this was the site of the free grammar school.

the Town House, first built in the twelfth century, and from the seventeenth century the home of the free grammar school. The higher one is Sunnyside, built in 1810, with a long garden at the back where one nineteenth-century owner charged the school £10 a year for the use of his privy. The last on the right, just before the churchyard, is the Old Manor House. In the middle years of the twentieth century this was lived in by a lady, Miss Butler, who had a dozen or more cats, not known for their high standards of hygiene.

On the south side of the churchyard there are several fine old houses. The oldest and most beautiful of them, probably older than the twelfth-century church, is now erroneously called the Priory. It was originally the home of the bailiff who looked after the interests of the owner of the town and manor of Charlbury, the abbey of Eynsham. Although the manor belonged to a succession of owners after the dissolution of the monasteries in Henry VIII's reign, Charlbury was always a thriving market town, proud of its independence. The privilege of holding a market weekly and an annual fair was granted by king Henry III in 1256. There is a street fair every September.

I like to think that Charlbury means the *burh*, or fortified place, of the *ceorls*, or free men, though a more modern etymology would have it the *burh* of an individual called Ceorl. In any case the little town has always maintained its dignity against the pretensions of aristocracy in general and the influence of the two great estates that hem it in on the east and the west in particular, Cornbury and Ditchley. Indeed the little town's history illustrates the proposition that while England was from the Norman conquest and indeed since Anglo-Saxon times largely parcelled out into great estates, whose owners were national and sometimes international figures, it was perfectly possible for purely local families to accumulate significant wealth and power.

To the east were the Lees of Ditchley, earls of Litchfield and ancestors of the Virginia Lees. To the west lies the Cornbury estate, which until the late nineteenth century belonged to the Churchill dukes of Marlborough, who move out of the splendours of Blenheim every summer into their lesser house of Lee Place in Charlbury to leave their palace to the tourists. Charlbury has always been defensive when confronted with the claims of the inhabitants of Cornbury, whose entrance lodge is just across the Evenlode from the town. Over the centuries, however, local families like the Spendloves and the Albrights have meant as much for the daily life of the town as the claims of the Lees and the Churchills, who were as often as not embroiled in debt or dangerous political quarrels.

As long ago as the reign of Queen Elizabeth the free men of Charlbury found themselves being treated like so many footballs by big money. Ownership of the manor and a tempting collection of financial properties and rights that went with it was disputed by St John's College, then as now one of the richest, if not *the* richest of the Oxford colleges, and two cronies of the Earl of Essex, Chamberlayne and Scudamore. The Queen seems to have handed Charlbury to her favourite, Essex, in a fit of absentmindedness, forgetting that she had already confirmed the Oxford college's ownership. Finally a group of yeomen and local gentlemen from Charlbury and the nearby villages of Fawler and Finstock pointed out that the transactions made over their heads took no notice of properties owned by local people 'before the memory of man'. And they got their way. Thomas Gifford, who had married a Chamberlayne girl and taken over Chamberlayne and Scudamore debts, made peace with the Charlbury '*ceorls*' by offering them a lease of valuable properties in Charlbury for 998 years at a peppercorn rent. Some of these still belong to the Gifford Trust, which manages them 'for the only use, profit and commodity of the tenants and inhabitants of Charlbury'.

From time to time the Churchills have attempted to treat Charlbury as an estate village. The present duke once claimed that he had the right to enter the church by his own private

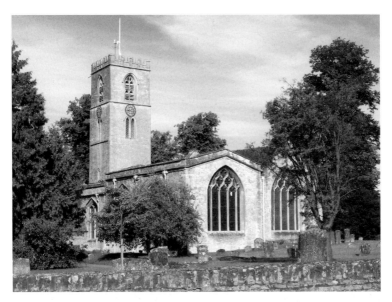

Charlbury's twelfth-century church of St. Mary the Virgin.

door, but the vicar refused to agree. For most of the nineteenth century Cornbury belonged to the Churchills and was used as a residence for the duke's oldest son, the Marquis of Blandford. Crippled with gambling debts, the Churchills had to sell Cornbury and it passed to a series of owners. The best loved was Vernon Watney, from the great London brewing family, who compiled and published a magnificent volume of historical research call *Wychwood and the Manor of Cornbury*. The present owner, the Lord Rotherwick, head of the Cayzer family, is less appreciated, in part because of their strenuous efforts to prevent Charlbury people from using paths through the forest of Wychwood that their forebears have used for centuries. These efforts included some fairly rough behaviour on the part of the present peer's father and his head gamekeeper, a former soldier servant, or batman, who was eventually convicted and served time for his bullying of walkers in the greenwood.

There are four surviving pubs in the town, of which the Bell and the Bull are most highly to be recommended. It was in the Bull that two friends from Washington, Daniel Patrick Moynihan (later senator from New York) and president Johnson's former special counsel, Harry McPherson, played hooky from a conference at Ditchley park to taste a pint of English bitter before their black tie dinner at the park. Moynihan, who spent quite a proportion of his three years at

The fountain in the Playing Close (far right) opened in 1900 to commemorate a visit from Queen Victoria and Arthur Albright's gift of a pure water supply. The Close was set aside for archery and other sports, including bull baiting, at least as early as 1447.

the London School of Economics on licensed premises, was anxious to show McPherson how much he was at home in an English country pub, and also how well he fitted in as a man of the people. But the two Americans were in evening dress. So when Moynihan asked the locals who were in possession of the dartboard in his best folksy manner if he and his friend could throw a few arrows, the locals grumbled. The rich, they were heard to say, always expected to have all the fun. The spirit of those Elizabethan yeomen lives on.

For many years Charlbury's chief occupation was gloving, and the town's leading citizens, master glovers by trade and Quakers by religion, were the Spendloves and the Albrights. The last glove factory closed in 1968, but there is a beautiful and well-attended eighteenth-century Quaker meeting house in Market Street. Like all small towns, Charlbury is struggling to preserve its independent amenities, and doing fairly well. The secondary school, the Spendlove School, of course, closed in the 1970s and has been replaced by the Spendlove Centre, with a medical centre, a vet and a Co-op opposite the ancient playing close, where the locals once practised archery. Barclays closed the only bank in town in the 1980s. (In its later years, the teller was Gaynor Regan, who married Tony Blair's first foreign secretary, Robin Cook.) Another notable modern resident was Dr. Rowan Williams, who continued to use a house in Market Street as a weekend refuge after his translation to the see of Canterbury in 2003.

In November 1910 a five-year-old boy arrived with his family to live in Cornbury, where his father had just been appointed head gardener by Vernon Watney. His name was Bill Campbell, and he became one of the most interesting and

— it is not too much to say — one of the most beloved citizens of Charlbury. Bill went to the primary school in Charlbury, and then on a scholarship to Oxford High School for Boys. He came back to Charlbury as a pupil teacher in 1925. After teacher training at Culham and a short stint in London, he came back in 1928 to teach at Charlbury School, where he taught science and developed a most unusually successful school garden, complete with beehives and poultry. Although he spent twenty-eight years in middle life at schools in Berkshire, he came back to Charlbury again when he retired, and for thirty years, from 1964 until shortly before his death at the age of 90 in 1994, Bill wrote a regular 'Country Diary' in *The Guardian*. He also broadcast regularly on both BBC Radio Oxford and the BBC World Service.

W. D. Campbell, as he signed his columns, though most people called him Bill and his closest friends called him Donald, was an all-round naturalist. He was a skilful and devoted gardener, expert in wildflowers, mammals and even fungi, and a devoted explorer of Wychwood. But his strongest suit was birds.

When he was about eighteen, one of the men working for his father at Cornbury found a bird caught and struggling in netting. The father recognized that it was a snipe, but sensed that there was something unusual about it, and suggested that Bill show it to Vernon Watney. Campbell said it was some kind of snipe. Watney was a scholarly man. (*Wychwood and the Manor of Cornbury*, privately printed, now sells for hundreds of pounds.) He looked the snipe up in his bird books, and told young Campbell to count its tail feathers. There were sixteen.

Charlbury from the hill above the Slade.

'Good gracious,' said Watney, 'it's a great snipe. The common snipe only has fourteen feathers.' It turned out that this was the first recorded in Oxfordshire since 1878. Campbell said he would let it go and Watney was pleased by the decision.

'At eight o'clock the next morning,' Campbell told his biographer, 'there was a knock at the door, and there was the postman with a parcel. It had been less than twenty-four hours since the great snipe had been released, when I was rewarded by the receipt of two books from Foyle's of London, C.A. Johns' *British Birds in their Haunts* and Aplin's *Birds of Oxfordshire*. It was the beginning of a lifelong fascination with birds, and the start of his acquisition of prodigious

Charlbury's eighteenth-century Quaker meeting house.
The Quakers have always been influential in the town.

detailed knowledge about their appearance, habitat, food and behaviour. In over sixty years he caught, ringed and released 60,000 birds of 110 species, and had his reward when 'his' birds were found and reported to him from virtually every country in Europe and from as far away as Israel, Morocco and the Congo.

Charlbury no longer has a secondary school. It does have a splendid newish primary school, sadly without a school garden (attended a quarter of a century ago by my two daughters), a bookshop, half a dozen other shops, a handsome community centre at the Corner House, a railway station, five places of worship (Church of England, Roman Catholic, Baptist, Methodist and Quaker), and a generally thriving community life. It even had its own newspaper. Professor Robert Leslie, head of history at Queen Mary College in London University, and his wife Margery, head of Richmond College, bought a house in Church Street in 1972 which they planned as a retirement home and used as a weekend cottage. Professor Leslie became a great friend of the Jesuit, Father Robert Bulbeck, who was the priest in charge of the Roman Catholic church in Charlbury. They called each other Holy Robert and Unholy Robert. Father Bulbeck persuaded Professor Leslie to start a local newspaper, which he did. He accumulated news through conversations with Charlburians, to a considerable extent by visiting Charlbury's numerous pubs. From 1990 to 1996, he composed it on an Amstrad word processor, and his wife helped him to take it to the printers and to distribute it. It was her death in 1996, it seems, that persuaded him to close the paper. The *Charlbury News* was written in a dry and humorous style. Leslie spent much effort in trying to encourage his fellow-citizens to compose limericks, whether the town's name was pronounced to rhyme with 'marl' or 'tall'. It came nearest to muckraking in its energetic passages dealing with the two dark clouds that shaded Charlbury's otherwise sunny life: litter and the occasional vandalism of the teenagers who hung out round the public toilets in the Spendlove centre. He reported, characteristically, that 'a senior citizen of some standing' was passing the centre when he noticed that

> the assembled youths, both male and female, were throwing items of litter around at random. He recommended to them that they should use the litter bins ... The young people replied in their local patois, which will need translation for

those unfamiliar with it ... They asked him to depart hetero-sexually or homosexually, adding that he was born out of wedlock.

These preoccupations attracted the notice of the national newspaper, *The Guardian*, which commented, in effect, that Charlbury should be so lucky. If beer cans in the car park and occasional jeering from teenagers were the worst the citizens had to fear, *The Guardian* mused enviously from its viewpoint in Farringdon Road, life in Charlbury sounded relatively idyllic. Without being too heavy-handed, it is possible to interpret Professor Leslie's imbroglio with the youth of Charlbury (for who can doubt that the editor was himself the 'senior citizen of some standing'?) as an incident in the transformation of the town from an agricultural society that offered few opportunities to its young to a refuge for the elderly, the confident and the genteel. After all, the archbishop of Canterbury, by definition an exemplar of respectability, had a weekend house in Charlbury, his privacy affectionately guarded by the town.

In recent years, as Professor Leslie recorded with irritation, the character of the town has indeed undeniably changed. Where once it was a country town, dependent on gloving and agriculture for a modest prosperity, it has become something of a dormitory town. Charlbury is only ten minutes and a few pounds by train from Oxford, and a significant number of commuters travel to and from the City of London by way of Paddington. An underground classic, *Notes from Over-ground*, by a Secret Service official called Roger Green, who commuted for decades from his home in Wolvercote to the Circus, commemorates the sufferings of this nomadic band.

(Improbably, Green now lives on the Greek island of Hydra, next to Leonard Cohen, and sports a great white beard. That would surely have been grounds for suspicion at the Circus.) Many academics from the two universities in Oxford, Oxford and Oxford Brookes, have come to live in Charlbury, and they contribute to the town's lively character. There are more academics in Charlbury now than there are glovers!

≈ TWELVE ≈

BEYOND Charlbury riverside perambulations become trickier, for a number of reasons. The Oxfordshire Way peels off and runs across country to the eastward on the line of the Roman road from Bath to St Alban's, Akeman Street, which crosses the Evenlode by a ford (now supplemented by a wooden bridge) in what has become the Stonesfield bathing place. The Cecils of Wilcote discourage walking on their estate, which owns the land on the right bank from the Charlbury-Witney road to Ashford Mill. And at this point the river runs through what is called, perhaps a little pretentiously, the Evenlode gorge. This is hardly a deep slash cut in the landscape, between beetling brows, like the Gorges du Tarn. But from Fawler to Ashford Mill, and again between the East End of North Leigh and Combe, the Evenlode runs through hanging woods, steep enough that the best path is often some distance from the river. In fact, the section from Charlbury past Fawler, Stonesfield and Combe to Long Hanborough is the shaggiest but for my taste the most beautiful part of the entire Evenlode valley.

Fawler is now no more than a hamlet. In the past it was more important, largely because of its iron ore deposits. The British Geological Survey first identified ironstone there in the 1850s, and the ore was mined both by opencast and underground mining until it was exhausted in the late-nineteenth century. Fawler is also the site of a Roman villa; it is said to be called after the *faganfloran*, the mosaic pavement of a Roman villa uncovered when the railway line was being built in 1852. This is only one of several Roman sites in the region. Recent excavation along Akeman Street between Ramsden and Wilcote has uncovered large quantities of Roman pottery and animal shards, suggesting the presence of a third-century McDonald's where travellers along the highway could refresh themselves with wine and meat. Holly Grove, the wood to the east of Wilcote, contains one of the most delightful walks in the whole district. The ancient coppice wood not only has a sea of bluebells in season but — if you know where to look for them, and I'm not telling you — wild bee orchids, which are quite common in the Evenlode valley. But Holly Grove, or the part of the wood called Coneygar, also has traces of mounds built by the Romans, as some say, or the Normans, to breed rabbits, which they introduced into Britain for food.

At Ashford Mill, instead of going up on the road through hanging woods to East End and down a lane to the villa, you can turn left and cross Stonesfield common, grazed by the miniature black Dexter cattle, to Stonesfield village. Stonesfield had a Roman villa of its own, a large house with a richly patterned mosaic floor in the manner associated with

Holly Grove has a carpet of bluebells in spring.

Above: The view south-east from Stonesfield Common.
Right: The wooden bridge that takes the footpath from Stonesfield over
the village swimming hole towards the North Leigh Roman villa at
East End is on the site of a ford that took Akeman Street
across the Evenlode on its journey from Cirencester to St Alban's.

Cirencester. The floor was uncovered in the eighteenth century, and subsequently destroyed, though there exists a tapestry, which shows what it was like. Stonesfield's principal recent literary association is with the Oxford don, poet and former Jesuit, Peter Levi – author of an elegant account of Hellas under the heel of the miserable colonels, *The Hill of Chronos* – who married Cyril Connolly's former wife, Deirdre.

*The tessellated pavement in the dining room of
the East End Roman villa.*

From Stonesfield there are a number of tempting walks.
Akeman Street heads eastward towards St Alban's across the
northern part of Blenheim Park, accessed by a high wooden
ladder over the park wall. You can also head back to
Charlbury by an ancient green track, the Saltway, which
runs past the pepperpot lodges to Ditchley park and heads
northwards through Taston. This was one of the routes by
which the precious salt from Cheshire saltpans reached the
Thames valley.

Those who want to follow the Evenlode, however, should
cross the river by the footbridge, bear half-left across a
meadow and up the hill along the traces of a demolished stone

wall as far as the North Leigh Roman villa. This was a substantial country house with sixty rooms, built round three sides of a court, with the opening to the south. The buildings remain up to a metre or so above ground. There is a fine tessellated floor, monochrome with dolphins, preserved under a roof. You can also see the remains of the hypocausts, Roman underfloor heating, in many of the rooms. This must have been the home of a wealthy landowner, probably not Roman in the sense of an immigrant from the Italian peninsular, but a Romano-Celtic gentleman converted to Roman tastes.

The site is managed by English Heritage, and some years ago I was told by the retired schoolmaster who was then the caretaker that he had found traces of vines, *vitis vinifera*, the wine-producing variety, on the slopes the other side of the railway from the villa. It is a nice thought, as is the local belief that the giant snail shells to be found along the river bank between Combe and Hanborough are of an edible variety introduced by the Romans.

Having duly inspected those ruins, you climb the hill to the right. You can go up a lane, or take a rougher path through the wood on your left, where there are traces of old quarrying, and a big badger sett. At the top you arrive at the parking place (sadly there are police warnings of thieves active there) and head to the left through East End.

The road is lined with modern houses, a typical 'suburb in search of a city' of a kind that is not uncommon in west Oxfordshire, but if you take any one of a number of marked footpaths between them, you come to an older line of stone houses. You head down hill through these, and a wonderful walk across the Evenlode valley to Combe opens up. As you descend, you have a choice. You can either follow a rough cart track that skirts the edge of the wood, or you can enter the wood and follow a stream downhill inside the tree line. Whichever path you take, you will come to a little bridge over a stream at the bottom, which takes you into a water meadow. Instinct would suggest that you go straight across. But in this case, as so often, instinct is wrong. You bear half left and cross the Evenlode on a substantial wooden bridge. On the other bank, you climb steeply for a few yards round the back of Grintley Hill cottage, and find yourself on a lane that heads up the far side of the valley into Combe. Half way up, you can look down from a high railway bridge onto a straight section of the OWW rail track.

Just outside Combe, you can look down from a high railway bridge on to a straight section of the OWW rail track.

Combe church across the village cricket pitch.

There is a possibility of a circular walk here. As you come into Combe village, known locally for some long-forgotten reason as 'Silly Combe', you can take a lane to the left. (It runs into another with the wonderful name of Chatterpie Lane.) That will take you through two farmyards to a gate where you turn hard left along the hedge until you find yourself on the bank of the Evenlode and eventually back at the North Leigh Roman villa. The circular walk is useful if you left the car at the parking place.

Those who take the golden journey to Long Hanborough will have rested for a moment in Combe. This is one of the nicest villages in Oxfordshire, with a village green and a cricket ground overlooked by a pretty church and a spreading cedar. It also has a primary school rated as one of the best in the whole country. Like Finstock, Combe boasts a 'halt' on the Great Western line, an unroofed platform where only one train in either direction stops each day. Opposite, on the site of the Domesday water mill, is the duke of Marlborough's sawmill, a cluster of stone buildings housing clanking Victorian machinery crowned by a miniature conical tower that would not be out of place in a Gascon *chateau fort*. Combe, or *cwm*, means 'valley', and since the middle ages it has migrated uphill from the riverside.

Just below the sawmill the Evenlode flows under the ancient Combe bridge and turns left towards the wall of Blenheim Park.

Combe bridge, upstream from 'Rupert's beach'. Over the centuries the village moved uphill from the cwm to a higher site on the edge of Blenheim park.

Our favourite place on the entire Evenlode, Rupert's Beach.

You can park in a short lane lined with lime trees beyond the bridge, pass under the railway line through a dank brick arch, climb a locked gate and find yourself on the edge of a vast field with the Blenheim woods on the other side of the river.

If you head diagonally to the left, in a hundred yards or less you come to one of our favourite places on the entire Evenlode, the place we called Rupert's Beach. It was a favourite of my dog Rupert, a Labrador-collie cross, who loved to splash in the water where it rounds a bend and a beach of hard sand made it easy for him to enter the water. Water from a spring on the far bank enters the river through a tiny cascade opposite the beach.

One day, filming with my son Pierre, who lives in Paris, we experienced one of those magic moments all film-makers hope to catch. He was making a film for the French market about the American Deep South during the civil rights movement, which I covered as a correspondent for *The Observer*, and he wanted to point up the contrast between that world and my life in retirement in West Oxfordshire. I suggested that we might do some filming in the field next to Rupert's beach. He put me on the river bank, with the Blenheim woods behind me. As Jérome, the cameraman, turned over, around the corner there sailed two swans, cob and pen, followed in single file by six fluffy grey cygnets. Nothing could have been more perfect. And if we had tried to take that shot deliberately, we could have shot it a hundred times and it would never have happened so perfectly again.

∽ THIRTEEN ∾

THE OTHER side of the river, the Blenheim woods come down close to the bank. The Blenheim wall here is somewhat dilapidated, and many of the ancient oaks in this part of the wood are dead, their branches stark against the sky. There are good walks in the park and the duke allows walkers to follow a path round the lake, one of the great Capability Brown's masterpieces, made by damming the river Glyme, which meets the Evenlode between Long Hanborough and Bladon. Again for those looking for a circular walk it is possible to cross a brick bridge just north of the Bladon to Hanborough road and head back towards Combe on the far bank. This is where the track is full of large, vaguely Burgundian snails, supposed by those with romantic imaginations to be descended from edible snails introduced by the Romans. Once when we were walking on this path the field was full of sheep. Suddenly an old dog fox emerged from the riverbank and walked casually a diagonal right through the sheep, through the hedge and up the hill until he passed out of sight. None of the sheep paid him the slightest attention.

At the south-western corner of Blenheim park the Glyme emerges from the lake into which Capability Brown had poured it and flows into the Evenlode, roughly opposite the entrance to the Long Hanborough station and the thriving industrial park that has grown up around it. This is the site of an ambitious project, finished in 2006, undertaken by the Environment Agency (heir to the National Rivers Authority and the Thames Conservancy) to enhance the quality of the Evenlode.

There were two motives. One was to improve the quality of the river as an environment for fish and other wildlife. The other was to reduce the risk of flooding downstream, and especially in and around Oxford, where aerial photographs in some winters showed miles of flooding. Both motives, and the decision to act on them, reflected a reversal of past priorities in relation to river management. In the context of the government's new sympathy to environmental concerns and biodiversity at the time of the Rio earth summit of 1992, the emphasis of policy shifted from land drainage to flood control only where towns and property were at risk. Now the Environment Agency was saying it wanted rivers to be as natural as possible.

The deterioration of the river's habitat quality, especially for fish, was largely due to the postwar dredging. Sites for spawning and backwaters and other refuges for young fish were lost and had become few in number. The answer was to slow the river down by introducing in effect artificial meanders. This would be good for fish, but it would also help many other species, including at the top of the food chain mammals such as otters and voles, and so on all the way down to the invertebrates and plankton at the bottom of it.

The project has involved extensive engineering work on a two-kilometre stretch of the Evenlode at the southern end of Blenheim park. Gravel would be dumped on both sides of the stream to create 'sidebars' and 'riffles'. This would make the river more sinuous, which in turn would make it more diverse as a habitat. New species of fish, such as barbel, would be encourage to breed there. At the same time the river's capacity would be reduced, in effect reversing the effect of earlier dredging that widened the profile of its bed.

This has been done. At the same time a 'two-stage channel' has been excavated in the meadows along the riverbank. Semi-circular bays have been dug, lying just above the normal summer water level, so that they would normally remain dry. But at times of spate flood water is encouraged to come over the bank further upstream than otherwise and to spill into these area. This would both provide additional storage for floodwater, protecting the riverside areas of Oxford from flooding, while incidentally creating refuges for young fish which would otherwise be washed downstream. The work was too little and perhaps too late to save Oxford from severe flooding in July 2007.

The engineering work occupies little more than a mile at Bladon, but its effect both on slowing down the 'flashy' flow of the river and consequently on the biodiversity of its environment will be felt for miles both upstream and downstream.

A few years ago otters, the biggest and most interesting of the riverside mammals of lowland England, were almost extinct in the Thames catchment area, though they were still fairly common in Dorset, Devon, Cornwall and on the Wye. They suffered both from direct poisoning from the organochlorine pesticides aldrin and dieldrin, and from the indirect effect of pollution on fish, their main food.

Since then the situation has improved. In the 169 sites surveyed in 1977-79, no otters or traces of otters were found. In 1984-86, the same was true. In 1991-94, there were four positive sightings. (Because otters are nocturnal, most sightings would be of 'spraints', or faeces, rather than of the animals themselves.) But in 2000-2002 18 out of 225 sites surveyed yielded positive results. In the Upper Thames region, including the Windrush and the Evenlode, there were no positives in any of the three earlier surveys, but there were signs of otters at ten out of the 32 sites in 2000-2002. Consolidation of the otter population seems to be taking place, according to the otter survey. One reason for this is that in 1999 the Otter Trust released six males and eleven females at three sites in the Upper Thames. Otter activity increased. Three cases of successful breeding are known, but at least seven of the animals released have been found dead on roads. However otters, which can travel considerable distances overland, are believed to have entered the Cotswold rivers from adjacent areas naturally. The future of this sleek predator on the Evenlode remains problematic, but they are back, even though you will be lucky to see one unless you get up in the middle of the night on purpose to look for them.

Penny Franklin, a nurse at the John Radcliffe hospital in Oxford who lives in Long Hanborough and has been a local councillor there, has worked with the Berkshire, Bucks and Oxfordshire Wildlife Trust (BBOWT) on their otter survey. She subsequently graduated to larger and fiercer mammals when she was given a grant to study black bears in the United States. Mrs Franklin was also surveying water voles, which are in even worse shape as a species than otters.

BBOWT estimates that the population of voles has fallen by 95 per cent since they featured as Ratty in Kenneth Grahame's classic, *The Wind in the Willows*, written in 1908. They are attempting to reverse this disastrous trend, and otters, which they are also hoping to protect, may be able to help them. While some of the decline in voles is due to habitat change, much of it is due to the depredations of the American mink, which have escaped from fur farms in the vicinity, and which prey on water voles. The incidental benefit is that otters will drive away mink. So the return of the otters should mean the return of Ratty too. There is a certain appropriateness about this, as Otter was Ratty's friend in Grahame's book.

❦ FOURTEEN ❦

EVEN today, in a supposedly democratic age, the influence of the house of Churchill in west Oxfordshire is
very great. For most of the last three hundred years, the
direct and collateral descendants of John Churchill, first
duke of Marlborough, have owned much of the Evenlode
valley and of the royal forests of Woodstock, Cornbury and
Wychwood. In the nineteenth century, the family owned not
only Blenheim palace, the biggest and arguably the most
splendid private house in England, but Cornbury as well.

When the duke is constrained to put his rents up, his deci-
sion is felt in farms and shops from Charlbury to Oxford. The
Evenlode's most important tributary, the Glyme, reaches its
banks after passing through Blenheim Park and Capability
Brown's great lake. Blenheim land marches with Ditchley as
far as Charlbury, and reaches as far as the northern suburbs of
Oxford. Street names in north Oxford — Sunderland Avenue,
Blandford Avenue — refer to the subordinate titles of the
Marlboroughs. Sir Winston Churchill was born in Blenheim
palace, and buried in the churchyard of Bladon church, whose
tower can be seen from the bank of the 'Bladon stream'. The
lower course of the Evenlode runs through Churchill territory.

The history of the Churchill family has been a strange
amalgam of glory and infamy.[6] The founder, John, first duke
of Marlborough, was the son of a Devon knight of no great
distinction. He was drawn into the dissolute court of Charles
II because his sister Arabella was a beauty at court and one of
the mistresses of James, duke of York, who succeeded his

101

brother to become king James II. Young Churchill, as a penniless ensign in the foot guards, was for a time the lover of Barbara Villiers, herself a discarded mistress of Charles II. Although his great descendant Winston Churchill spent years writing a four volume life of his ancestor to disprove what he regarded as the disgraceful libels on his family of the great Whig historian, Lord Macaulay, it is plain that John Churchill was — as Macaulay put it — 'not less distinguished by avarice and baseness than by capacity and valour'.

Capable and courageous he certainly was. He stands with Cromwell and Wellington as one of the very greatest of British captains. He defeated the victorious armies of Louis XIV in half a dozen pitched battles, not least because of the daring and skill of his lightning manoeuvres. But he, and his wife Sarah, were undeniably avaricious. The Blenheim estate itself, one of the choicest morsels in the gift of a king of England, was only the crowning achievement of their relentless search for estates, lands, titles, honours and money.

As for baseness, there is little doubt that the young Churchill was the kept lover of Barbara Villiers, Lady Castlemaine, later the duchess of Cleveland. She paid him so handsomely for his favours that he was able to invest in an annuity that, without making him rich, did give him independence. That was not perhaps so very disgraceful in the eyes of a dissolute and cynical court. Barbara Castlemaine does not perhaps deserve Macaulay's epithets. 'This man', he wrote in the full moral confidence of a Victorian evangelical, 'who

The palace is seen framed by the branches of one of the magnificent cedars which stand on the north-west side of the lake.

owed his rise to his sister's dishonour, who had been kept by the most profuse, imperious and shameless of harlots' was a 'prodigy of turpitude'. The harlot in question was a royal mistress, not seen in the seventeenth century (or indeed in the twenty-first) as a wholly dishonourable status. She was also a descendant of the marriage between the son of Sir George Villiers and the daughter of Sir John St. John, two country gentlemen of the reign of James I. The offspring of that union included, among many other brilliant and famous people, Winston Churchill, the Pitts, father and son, both prime ministers, their rival Charles James Fox, the novelist Henry Fielding and Viscount Grey of Fallodon, foreign secretary, bird watcher and fly fisherman. (W.D. Campbell had an anecdote about Grey asking him, as a boy, to pass him his 'lending net'. It took Campbell a moment to think this was not the opposite of a borrowing net, but a landing net.) From this 'great Villiers connection', wrote John Maynard Keynes, are descended 'all the ambitious fascinators, with so much charm of countenance and voice and so hard a little nut somewhere inside', a perfect description both of the Villiers women, royal mistresses in Stuart times, and of Winston Churchill and his great ancestor, John duke of Marlborough. This, wrote Keynes, 'is indeed the real blood royal of England'.[7]

What is harder to justify is Marlborough's conduct towards James II, who had made him, and whom he betrayed. James had given his brother's former mistress's bold and tough lover high and well-remunerated office at court and a peerage, and finally placed him in command of his Guards. Whether because in spite of everything religious scruples made him jib at becoming a Catholic, or because he foresaw that only born

Catholics would prosper at James's court, or simply out of an eye for the main chance, Churchill entered into secret negotiations with William of Orange's diplomatic envoy, Everard Van Dykvelt. William landed at Torbay with his giant Swedish grenadiers in bearskins and his veteran Dutch troopers accompanied by African servants, under a banner inscribed with the motto of the House of Orange, *Je Maintiendrai*, I will maintain, to which he had added his political slogan: 'the Liberties of England and the Protestant Succession'.

It was at this moment that Churchill betrayed him. After a council of war at which he realized that he was under suspicion, he slipped away by night to join the invader. He left an abject letter, protesting his personal loyalty to James, but explaining that his protestant principles made treason unavoidable. His wife and her bosom friend, the princess Anne, slipped away too, down the backstairs of the palace at night in dressing gown and slippers. The bishop of London, Henry Compton, who was another conspirator, saw them to safety, dressed in the buff coat he had worn in the life guards a generation earlier and armed with sword and pistols.

At this drastic moment of the Glorious Revolution, which did indeed establish the liberties of England and the protestant succession, not to mention the fortunes of the 'Venetian oligarchy' of Whig grandees who would run the country for the next two centuries, there was a west Oxfordshire coincidence. The young Viscount Cornbury, heir to the earl of Clarendon and to Wychwood, commanded a regiment of the king's dragoons. He too betrayed James. He put himself at the head of three regiments and tried to take them over to William. He aroused suspicion, and in the end joined William almost alone.

John Churchill's fortune was made. William made him first earl of Marlborough, then marquis of Blandford. In 1704 after a pelting forced march, he won his great battle at Blindheim on the upper Danube which the English called Blenheim. His grateful sovereign, who happened to be his wife's best friend, Anne, made him a duke, and granted lands that had been the favourite hunting grounds of the kings of England since Anglo-Saxon times: the manor of Woodstock and the Hundred of Wootton. That added up to 22,000 acres.

Queen Elizabeth, as a young princesss suspected of complicity in Wyatt's rebellion, was imprisoned at Woodstock in 1554-55. She later handed it over to Sir Henry Lee of Ditchley,

The bridge over the lake at Blenheim.

founder of the fortunes of the Lee family who went on to glory in Virginia. The Marlboroughs, to this day, do not own Blenheim in freehold. They pay a quitrent to the crown of a French flag with three fleurs-de-lys once a year.

Urged on and prompted by the sheer will of duchess Sarah, the great captain set out to build himself a worthy home. He commissioned Sir John Vanbrugh, playwright and stage designer, to built a paradigm of baroque glory. There were endless rows about money, unpaid bills, a nasty quarrel with the architect, but in the end it was finished. Over the great gate the proud legend was inscribed.

> Under the auspices of a munificent sovereign this house was built for John Duke of Marlborough, and his Duchess Sarah, by Sir J Vanbrugh between the years 1705 and 1722. And this Royal manor of Woodstock, together with a grant of £240,000, towards the building of Blenheim was given by Her Majesty Queen Anne and confirmed by Act of Parliament...

It was, and is, a trumpet blast of a house. But not even the revenues of the princely estate that went with it kept the Churchill and Spencer Churchill descendants from financial problems. The later history of the Churchills strangely follows the double legacy of the founder of their glory.

The fifth duke was compelled to sell off a famous library as well as his estate at Whiteknights, on the outskirts of Reading, now the site of the university there. The Cornbury estate passed to relations, who had the title of Lord Churchill, and for a time the Cornbury estate was known as the Blandford estate, after the honorary title of the heir to the duchy of Marlborough. But in the middle of the nineteenth century that had to be sold. The sixth duke had astronomical gambling debts. Another duke had to sell off a fabulous collection of paintings. The seventh duke was so broke that he had to be bailed out with the Blenheim Settled Estates Act of 1880, which broke the entail on the Blenheim estate and enabled him to sell off precious heirlooms like the Sunderland library of 18,000 volumes, Raphael's 'Ansidei Madonna' and Van Dyck's equestrian painting of Charles I, both now in the National Gallery, London.

The eighth duke, known as the marquis of Blandford for most of his life, because he died shortly after inheriting the dukedom, was described by the historian David Cannadine as 'one of the most disreputable men ever to have debased the highest rank in the British peerage'. No wonder that William Gladstone, no enemy to the aristocracy, said he had never met a Churchill who had either morals or principles.

The brother of the reprobate eighth duke, however, was the great Lord Randolph Churchill, who died of syphilis, but might have been prime minister himself had he not miscalculated the consequences of a tactical resignation. He was married to an American heiress, Jenny Jerome, daughter of a somewhat raffish stock market speculator and horse-racing punter, Leonard Jerome. Lord Randolph and his wife Jenny were the parents of Winston Churchill, born in 1874.

Several other Marlboroughs 'gilded their coat of arms', as the French say, by seeking a well-endowed American bride, including the ninth duke, who married Consuelo Vanderbilt. That marriage ended in divorce, but the duke then married another American heiress, Gladys Deacon from Boston, who was a friend of the great art collector, Bernard Berenson and of such French artists as Rodin and Degas. She had a famous affair at Blenheim with the crown prince of Germany.

In the 1890s, the dukes, in spite of their chronic impecuniosity, lived in tremendous style. They employed an indoors staff of about 40, and 50 or so out of doors, including dairy maids, electricians, carpenters, gardeners, a cricket professional, a night watchman, and lodge-keepers and gamekeepers in livery.

In the first world war Blenheim was used as a hospital, but it was World War II that brought the old ducal lifestyle to an end. First the boys from Malvern public school moved in, and when they moved out MI5, the security service, took over. The counter-intelligence staff reached a total of 1,000.

Even today, though, Blenheim remains a gigantic enterprise. The estate still owns 11,500 acres, of which 5,500 acres are let to 20 tenant farmers and 3,900 acres (including the park of 2,400 acres) are farmed by the estate 'in hand'. The estate also owns 1,550 acres of woodland and 128 cottages and houses, not to mention the famous Bear Hotel in Woodstock, or the mineral water bottling plant, the garden centre, toy railway, and the sawmill. So many tourists flock round that from time to time the duke and duchess move out to a less splendid but still beautiful home, Lee Place in Charlbury. The Churchill family have perhaps lost more money than any other of the great British landed families. But there is still a lot left; £185 million, according to the *Sunday Times* 'rich list'. Indeed, a hundred years after the Churchills married into the Vanderbilts because they needed the $2.5 million in railway stock that made up Consuelo's dowry, it is entirely possible that the Churchills are now richer than the Vanderbilts.

What does this have to do with the Evenlode? Well, the dukes of Marlborough own more of the land the Evenlode flows through than anyone else, and they have had, and still have, more influence over the people who live along its banks.

≈ FIFTEEN ≈

WHERE THE Evenlode, or perhaps here we should call it the 'Bladene stream', reinforced by the Glyme, slides past the artificial bars of the Blenheim enhancement scheme, it is on its home stretch, only five miles or so from its merger with the Thames. We have only tentatively explored these last miles, often glimpsed from the windows of the train, where the Evenlode meanders through fields reminiscent of the Midlands. Circumstances, as they say, beyond my control have prevented me from walking this last lap of the river's course. It is also true that this last stage is hard to walk. There are no footpaths along either bank, and the farmers have put up fierce notices forbidding access. Below Hanborough is the site of Hanborough mill, and after skirting a wood, the river describes a whole circle, the Burleigh Loop, as if it was on the point of creating a horseshoe lake.

This last stretch of the river runs through a shallow valley between two ridges, with the spire of Church Hanborough, half a mile or so south of Long Hanborough, to the west, and the ridge crowned by Burleigh farm, site of a spectacular rick fire a few years ago, to the east. Perhaps because of its inaccessibility, the reach that passes Goose Eye farm is one of the most attractive stretches of the river, if you can get to see it. It winds placidly through meadows, flanked by big willow trees, well away from the road, with no continuous riverside path.

That leads to Eynsham mill, which was for a while the Isis fish farm, which is well outside Eynsham. Downstream there is a riverside path for a while. Now we are almost on the A40, with its Oxford commuters and its trucks, many of them now from eastern Europe, heading for Cheltenham, South Wales and the Irish ferry at Fishguard.

There is one more mill, Cassington mill, which in Domesday paid a rent of 175 eels a year.[8] Alas! There are now virtually no eels here or anywhere in the Evenlode; their numbers have fallen to less than one per cent of what they were once, according to the experts at the Environment Agency. Eel runs are a thing of the past on the Thames and its tributaries above the Goring Gap. From the A40 the area now looks wholly lost to industrial development. There is a Mercedes truck dealership and a caravan park. But if you approach Cassington mill from the Eynsham to Cassington road, which is cut off at the A40 in a dead end, you are in a strange limbo. You can hear the roar of the traffic, but the fields the Evenlode crosses on its last lap are unspoiled. Wharf Farm is close to the site of Cassington mill, which was a working flour mill until 1938. From there a disused canal, as straight as a knife, runs half a mile or so down to the Thames. It was built by a nineteenth-century duke of Marlborough to ship out produce and ship in coal and building materials. There the Evenlode turns eastward to debouch into the Thames.

Less than a mile above that spot is Swinford bridge, where the B4044, the road that circles Oxford outside the ring road on the west, crosses the Thames at Eynsham. This is, astonishingly, one of fewer than a dozen toll bridges left on public roads in England, and one of only two on the Thames. There every morning and evening long lines of blaspheming commuters wait to hand over a five penny coin to thrusting hands poked out of a sort of sentry box in the middle of the road. Tolls have been charged for crossing the Thames here for more than a thousand years, first for a ford, then for a ferry, and since 1767 for a bridge. The bridge was built by the fourth earl of Abingdon, allegedly on the urging of George III because the farmer monarch had got his feet wet or at least had been afraid that he might. By 'an act for building a bridge cross the Thames' at Swinford, then in Berkshire, of [7] George III, c. 63, the earl was granted permission to charge two pence from every traveller using his new bridge, a fine balustraded structure of six arches.

And so things continued for a couple of centuries. The bridge now belongs to a Mr Michael Hawley and is managed by David and Sue Jackson and their team of collectors. They are generous about allowing local charities to bring plastic buckets and collect from the motorist waiting to cross the bridge. But local feeling has resented the bridge, and England being what it is, have continued to blame the earl for their inconvenience even after a commoner was responsible. In 1994 the owner sought to increase the toll from two pence to five, and efforts were made to abolish the toll. The legal action went all the way up to the House of Lords. But it lost there, and motorists still have to pay. Since the middle '90s, however, there has been a massive increase in population in Witney, especially, and many of those who live in Witney, Eynsham and surrounding villages work in Oxford every day. Every day 10,000 vehicles use the bridge.

Under these overhanging branches the sweet Evenlode loses its identity in the poet's 'sweet Themmes'.

In 2006 a painter, Jane Tomlinson, started through her blog what was initially a one-woman campaign to abolish the toll. At first local councillors told her that nothing could be done, and she felt she was being fobbed off when she tried to enlist the help of the Witney MP, David Cameron. She got a petition together. Whether it was the blog or the petition, things began to change. Councillors who had thought there was no way of building a new bridge, because this was forbidden by the Act of 1767, agreed to meet Ms. Tomlinson. David Cameron broke his silence and responded in a most encouraging way. 'I am

113

willing,' he wrote, 'to campaign for the Act of Parliament needed to buy the bridge and scrap the toll. I have made this clear to the county council, but they don't feel that's the way forward. It's a difficult and complicated situation, and I sympathise with people frustrated by the delays. I use the bridge myself, and find it frustrating. It does seem frankly rather strange to have to queue up and pay 5p.'

To reach the spot on the Thames path, which here runs on the south side of the river, and come opposite the mouth of the Evenlode, is complicated. You start from the car park of the Red Lion and follow a footpath along the side of the Siemens electronics factory. At the end of the building, following the Wharf stream, you go through a kissing gate into a field and pass through two fields. You have to climb two stiles before you reach a footbridge. Once over that, you head diagonally backwards towards Swinford lock. You cross the weir by

The sign reading 'Thames Conservancy RIVER EVENLODE' is half-obscured by the foliage of high summer.

another footbridge, and then the lock over its gates. Now you are on the Thames Path, and after about a mile you will see a sign recording that the stream pouring in from the north is the Evenlode.

 SIXTEEN

*Nessun maggior dolore che ricordarsi
del tempo felice nella miseria.*

SO SAID the ghost of Francesca da Rimini in Dante's fifth canto: that there is 'no greater sorrow than to remember in misery the happy time'. With the greatest respect to Francesca and to the poet, I have learned that the reverse is true. There is no greater joy available in a time of misery than to remember a happy time.

One afternoon, about eighteen months ago, I signed off on one book, and wrote the last pages of another. I stood up, planning to celebrate a successful afternoon's work, tripped over a cable, and ruptured the tendons of both knees. In some pain, I was taken to hospital, where my knees were restitched. While I was there, the doctors discovered a life-threatening infection. Again, I was successfully operated on, but I was weakened. It will be a long time before I can walk the last four or five miles of the river bank, from Bladon to Cassington mill and the Thames. Realistically, I may never be able to manage it. But in a hospital bed, unable to move, and still today, hobbling round the house, to remember the *tempo felice* of our walks along the Evenlode is anything but dolorous. To remember those explorations of our little river was a consolation and a joy.

The toll house at Swinford bridge, where a quiet river
meets fuming motorists.

After four hundred pages rich with history and philosophy, Claudio Magris and his Danube finally reached the Black Sea. They passed through the delta, where the river finally expires. It is 'a death that is incessant regeneration, an exuberance of plants and animals, reeds and herons, sturgeon, wild boar and cormorants, ash-trees and canebrakes, a hundred and ten species of fish and three hundred species of birds — a laboratory of life and the forms of life'.

We have herons and brown trout, and what I would call a quiet exuberance of birds, fish and animals. The nearest sturgeon are in the Bristol Channel, and they are rare enough, and the last wild boar were speared sometime around the end of the thirteenth century, though like the otters and the voles, but unlike the native crayfish, wild boar may return to the Oxfordshire woods.

The Danube flows through its delta in several channels. The central one has been corseted into a canal that ends in the port of Sulina, amid abandoned shipyards. 'A haphazard, colourless process of modernization has demolished the old Turkish town'. As a deathbed, it is not promising. But in the end the canal runs, 'calmly and confidently', into the sea.

> 'It is no longer a canal, a limitation . . . but a flowing outwards that opens and abandons itself to all the waters and oceans of the entire globe and to the creatures living in their depths. Lord let my death — says a line of Marin's[9] — be like the flowing of a river into the great sea.'

The Evenlode dies less dramatically. A few yards north of the A40, as if it were some indignity in a terminal ward, it is crossed by sewage pipes. Its last mile is peaceful, but then it pours its waters, not into a sea, but into the Thames. It has had a good life, and so no doubt have the little creatures living in and along its unpretentious bed. It has flowed almost unnoticed through the heart of England. Great deeds have been done there occasionally, and quiet lives, for the most part, lived on its banks, which still offer walks of contemplative pleasure.

Sweet Evenlode run softly till I end my song!

NOTES

1 It runs through Germany, Austria, Croatia, Hungary, Slovakia, Serbia, Bulgaria, Romania and Ukraine.

2 Robert Catesby sold the house to Walter Jones in 1601 to raise the money to pay the fine imposed on hi for his part in the Essex rebellion. The house was therefore started in about 1603, the year Queen Elizabeth died and James I succeeded, which is why I have called it Jacobean.

3 See Claire Tomalin, *Jane Austen, a Life*, London, Viking, 1997.

4 See Beryl Schumer, *Wychwood: The evolution of a wooded landscape*, Charlbury, Wychwood Press, 1999.

5 Margaret Gelling and Doris Mary Stenton, *The Place-names of Oxfordshire*, Part One, p. 7, English Place-name Society, Cambridge, Cambridge University Press.

6 The following account is based on Roy Jenkins, *Churchill*; Macaulay, *History of England*, vol I; David Cannadine, *Aristocracy*; W.S. Churchill, *Life of Marlborough*.

7 J.M. Keynes, 'The Great Villiers Connection', in *Essays in Biography*, London, Mercury, 1961.

8 I am indebted to Gordon Ottewell, *The Evenlode, an exploration of a Cotswold river*, Kencot, Green Branch, 2004, for much information in this last section and for his admirable maps, drawn by Pat Grover.

9 Biagio Marin, Italian poet, born Trieste 1891, and a favourite of his compatriot Claudio Magris.

INDEX

119

120

121